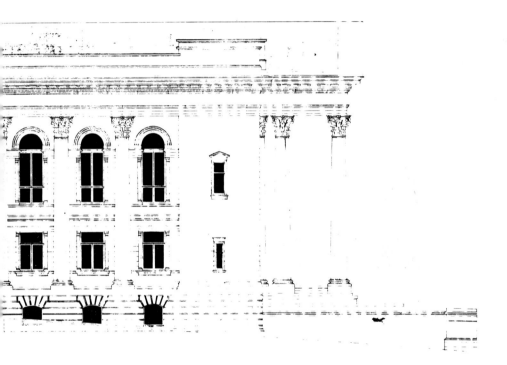

ᴀɴɴ Sᴛʀᴇᴇᴛ

3ₒ   4ₒ   5ₒ   6ₒ FEET.

WELLINGTON
CHURCH OF SCOTLAND
1884 – 1984

A history to mark the centenary of the opening in 1884
of the present Church buildings in University Avenue, Glasgow.

PUBLISHED BY THE CONGREGATION

ISBN   0 9510470 0 0

COVER PHOTOGRAPH
Hillhead viewed from the University Tower, 1937.
(Note Hillhead House on back cover)
Photo: *Courtesy* T. & R. Annan & Sons Ltd.

Printed by
H. B. Langman & Company Limited, 84-86 York Street, Glasgow G2 8LE.

Contents

List of Illustrations

Foreword

Thank God our time is now, when wrong
Comes up to face us everywhere,
Never to leave us till we take
The longest stride of soul men ever took.
Affairs are now soul-size.
The enterprise
Is exploration into God.

Christopher Fry: *A Sleep of Prisoners*

We thank God for the heritage that is ours in Wellington Church in 1984. We look back through the telescope of these pages to times when faith seemed more assured and confidence easier to come by. Theirs was a remarkable commitment, the men and women of Wellington's yesterday: and we are in their debt.

Our time is now. Now is the name of the time God has given to us. Not the yesterdays He gave to our fathers and mothers; nor the tomorrows He will give to our children. To us He has given the now of it. Because affairs are now soul-size: they demand the longest stride of soul men ever took. Our purpose is exploration into God and the place is where we are.

Ian Rodger, one of our Elders and a former Preses, has told a stirring story: it's the story of our city, of our Presbyterian tradition and of Wellington's place in this city and in that tradition. Without his story we would be rootless, in a time that knows its need of roots. We are grateful for the faithful telling of a story that is itself full of faith.

But the story is an empty tale, until it inspires us to match the faithful obedience of yesterday with the commitment that faith in Christ calls for today. For our enterprise is nothing less than exploration into God. Let us explore together in the work and the witness and the worship of Wellington. And let us thank God that our time is now.

Maxwell Craig
Minister of Wellington
March 1985

v

Preface

On 3rd October 1876 at the Annual Ordinary General Meeting of the male members of the congregation of Wellington Street United Presbyterian Church, the Preses, Mr. J. B. Kidston, in the course of his remarks drew attention to an Order issued by the Police Board of Glasgow declaring that from and after 1st January 1877 they would refuse all further applications for interment in the church crypt.

A year later, the Annual Meeting heard from their Preses that "the possible necessity of removing the church" to a more suitable locality had been mooted, and after discussion a motion was adopted, "that it be remitted to the Managers to take the matter into consideration and to ask a conference with the Session, with power to take such measures as they and the Session may jointly agree upon with a view to ascertaining the mind of the Congregation."

That conference duly met and considered a report showing the distribution of the congregation, which revealed that:–

255	(22%)	lived south of the Clyde
103	(9%)	lived in the east of the city
131	(12%)	lived in Anderston, south of Argyle Street
163	(14%)	lived in Anderston, north of Argyle Street
489	(43%)	lived on the west side of the city
1,141	100%	

410 lived within a half-mile radius of the church, but 630 within a similar circle centred on Charing Cross.

As a result, a Special General Meeting was called on 3rd December 1877, when the following Resolution was passed:–

1. "That in view of the changes which are going on in the residences of the population of our city and suburbs, especially in a direction westwards from our existing church, it seems prudent that the Congregation, although happily as yet uninjured by such changes, should look forward to a time, perhaps not far distant, when it might be their duty to make a change in their place of worship such as might at once be most suitable and convenient for their existing members or the greatest number of them, and for the permanent stability and edification of its membership";

2. "That meantime and in order to the congregation being free to entertain any proposal of a change which would involve as a preliminary the sale of their present place of worship, it is of importance to ascertain what rights may exist in the person of individuals as holders of lairs in the crypt underneath the church and how far such rights might be acquired or obviated and in what manner and on what terms, in order to the congregation being at liberty to dispose of the church and premises and so as to obtain the full value";

3. "That with the same view it further seems desirable meantime and under the unprecedented rise in the value of ground in and around Glasgow and the prospect of increased demand for such ground, that enquiry should be made as to the position and prices of such portion or portions thereof as may seem suitable and eligible to be purchased with a view to its becoming the site of a future place of worship for the congregation";

4. "That without anticipating the judgment of the congregation on the question of removal, a committee be appointed with a request that they make enquiries on the points brought out in the above resolutions, and report the result in due time to the congregation for their information and disposal"; and

5. "That the following members of the congregation be a committee . . . for the above purposes, viz. Dr. James Mitchell, Messrs. David Rowan, John Fairley, Archibald Arrol, Alex. A. Cuthbert, A. G. Hood, Anthony Hannay, J. B. Kidston, Alexander Allan, Matthew Slessor, William Shaw, Dr. M. Thomas, and R. S. Brown . . ."

This "Removal Committee" set about its responsible task immediately.

THE CENTENARY LOGO

The Story of the Congregation to 1884

The celebrations of 1984 mark one hundred years of the congregation's life and work in the present church. The story of the congregation itself, however, began in the events leading to 1792 and in the succeeding years before the move to the present building was undertaken. There will be another milestone on that road in 1992, the congregation's bicentenary, in only a few years time, and it is not easy, therefore, to decide how much of Wellington's story to recount here.

There are already several books, and the celebrations of 1992 will require to be chronicled in due course.

In 1877, there was printed "Some Annals of the United Presbyterian Congregation of Wellington Street, Glasgow". That history of the Congregation which was celebrating the jubilee of fifty years in the Wellington Street Church serves as a precedent for making a record linked to an anniversary of the building.

In March 1893, there followed an "Historical Sketch of Wellington United Presbyterian Congregation, Glasgow, 1792-1892, with an account of the proceedings in connection with the celebration of the centenary of the congregation and of the Rev. Dr. Black's Semi-Jubilee as its minister", (the obvious forerunner for 1992).

Then came two less comprehensive volumes. 1904 brought an "Account of the Proceedings in connection with the celebration of the Jubilee of the Rev. James Black, D.D., Senior Minister of Wellington United Free Church, 1854-1904", and in 1934 a book provided "A record of the proceedings at the celebration of Fifty Years of Worship in the Church in University Avenue, 1884-1934".

Since the story of the congregation of Woodlands Church is now merged with our own, it is right to note that "Woodlands United Presbyterian Church – Jubilee Memorial 1840-1890" was published in 1891.

A Brief Review of Early Days

The Presbyterian Church dates from the Reformation and particularly from the National Covenant and the Solemn League and Covenant. In the eighteenth century, about the time of the '45 Rebellion, there was an

1

attempt to form a National Church on an ecumenical basis, and the Secession Church stood out against what they saw as a dangerous watering-down of principles. Our roots go back to its Shuttle Street (Greyfriars) Congregation which met in the High Street near the Old College (neighbours of the University even then). In 1747, in protest against the Burgess Oath[1] of the day, with its reference to the established Church of the time, an Anti-Burgher section of the Secession Church withdrew from Shuttle Street to a room in The Cow Loan, later to become Queen Street. It is believed to have been close to where the equestrian statue of the Duke of Wellington now stands. They moved from there in 1754 to the Havannah Street-Duke Street corner. It was the only congregation in the Glasgow neighbourhood of the Anti-Burgher section of the Secession Church.

That meeting house became too small to contain a growing membership, and in 1792 a Petition for disjunction was presented to Presbytery by members "resident in Anderston, Partick, Meikle Govan and up the Water of the Kelvin" to form a separate "Associate Congregation of Anderston", then a salubrious suburb, not taken within the boundaries of Glasgow until 1846, whose folk were engaged in handloom weaving, bleaching, and cotton spinning, and "where trout rose on a summer's evening at the Broomielaw".

It was the time of the opening of the Forth & Clyde Canal – the Kelvin Aquaduct dates from 1787-90 – and the first connection by coach direct to London via Carlisle. Works were in hand to deepen the Clyde using the scouring force of the river itself. The old tobacco trade was in decline after the American War of Independence, but linen, leather, iron, glass, and household goods were being shipped overseas. The Chamber of Commerce, the first in the Commonwealth, was founded in 1783. It was a time of primitive agriculture and much famine and disease. Robert Burns was near his death. Burke, Pitt and Hastings were famous names. The French Revolution and the "reign of terror" was on its way. The population of Glasgow and its suburbs including Gorbals and Anderston was about 67,000 and that of the Anderston neighbourhood about 4,000.

On 5th November 1792 the new congregation was formed and on 26th December they adopted their constitution. The story of the other portion of the congregation, which continued in the Duke Street vicinity, and how their successors became the congregation of Woodlands Church who were united (or reunited) with Wellington in 1974, is told later in this volume.

In Cheapside Street, running down to the river from Argyle Street (remembered later as the scene of the terrible whisky bond fire in 1960 when 19 firemen perished) the Associate Congregation had already built a square meeting house with a burial ground enclosed by a stone wall. Originally

1. "I profess and allow with my heart the true religion presently professed within this realm, and authorised by the laws thereof"

there were 530 seats but this was increased to 983 when galleries were added in 1810. Some pews were sold outright and became the property of the members; others were let. Later on, a tent had to be erected on the grass to accommodate the overflow from the summer Communion.

On 1st August 1793, Dr. John Mitchell was called as the first minister, by 53 members and 35 "hearers", with no ladies allowed to sign. The stipend was £80. The Rev. Andrew Mitchell of Beith, his father, was present and the Mitchell family has been in continuous membership ever since. His grandson Andrew James Alexander Mitchell was at the opening services in 1884 and his great grand-daughter Eileen Anne Mitchell is a faithful member today.

There was of course no organ or other musical instrument (that came in 1884) and a precentor was appointed to lead the singing.

The first wedding was of Henry Bell, whose little steam paddler *Comet* was the pioneer of the Clyde steamers; her first captain was buried in the church's burial ground.

The congregation quickly established a Sunday School and from the beginning developed a strong missionary spirit, giving active support to the London Missionary Society and the British and Foreign Bible Society. In

CHEAPSIDE STREET MEETING HOUSE

DIVISIONS AND RE-UNIONS IN

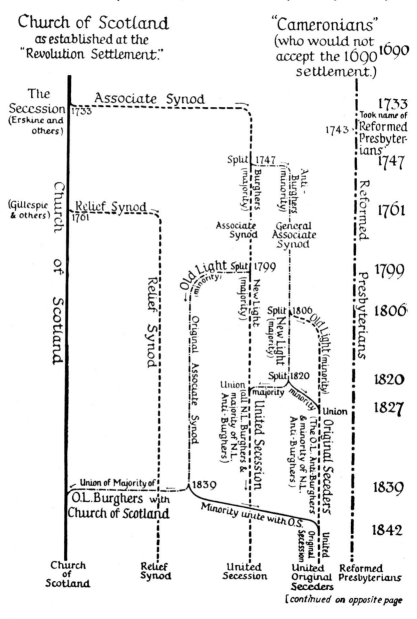

Church of Scotland
as established at the
"Revolution Settlement."

"Cameronians"
(who would not
accept the 1690
settlement.)

1690

The Secession (Erskine and others) 1733

Associate Synod

1733
Took name of
Reformed
Presbyterians.
1743

1747

Church of Scotland

Split 1747

Burghers (majority)

Anti-Burghers (minority)

(Gillespie & others) 1761

Relief Synod

1761

Associate Synod

General Associate Synod

Reformed Presbyterians

1761

Relief Synod

Old Light Split (minority) 1799

New Light (majority)

Original Associate Synod

1799

Split 1806

New Light (majority)

Old Light (minority)

1806

Split 1820

majority

minority

1820

Union 1827

Union (all N.L. Burghers & minority of N.L. Anti-Burghers)

United Secession

Original Seceders (The O.L. Anti-Burghers & minority of N.L. Anti-Burghers)

1827

Union of Majority of O.L. Burghers with Church of Scotland 1839

1839

Minority unite with O.S.

Original Secession

United Original Secession

1842

Church of Scotland

Relief Synod

United Secession

United Original Seceders

Reformed Presbyterians

[continued on opposite page

Scottish Presbyterianism

continued from opposite page]

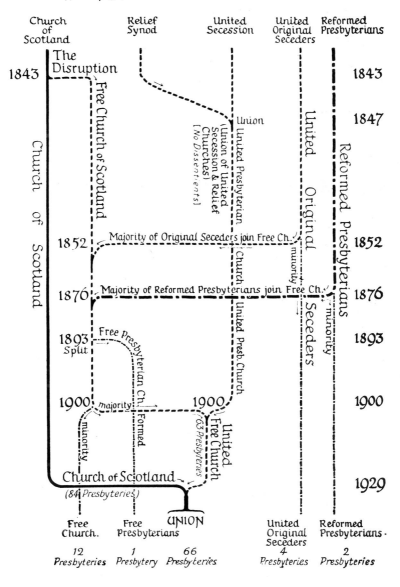

Church of Scotland | Relief Synod | United Secession | United Original Seceders | Reformed Presbyterians

1843 The Disruption

Church of Scotland

Free Church of Scotland

United Presbyterian Church (Union of United Secession & Relief Churches) [No Dissentients]

United Original Seceders minority

Reformed Presbyterians

1843

Union **1847**

1852 Majority of Original Seceders join Free Ch. **1852**

1876 Majority of Reformed Presbyterians join Free Ch. **1876**

United Presb. Church

1893 Free Presbyterian Ch Formed Split **1893**

1900 majority minority **1900** United Free Church 763 Presbyteries **1900**

Church of Scotland (84 Presbyteries)

1929

UNION

Free Church.	Free Presbyterians		United Original Seceders	Reformed Presbyterians.
12 Presbyteries	1 Presbytery	66 Presbyteries	4 Presbyteries	2 Presbyteries

5

WELLINGTON STREET CHURCH

1804 they embarked on the education of poor children, and this invaluable work continued until state education came with the Education Act of 1872.

In 1820 the slow process of reconciliation began when the two Secession Churches joined to form the United Secession Church.

After 35 years came the first move to a new location and a larger building. A site was found close to, but well to the west of, the city centre with "forbidding approaches across fields, but a good road could be made from Argyle Street". Waterloo was past, the name Wellington was on everyone's lips, and at the south-west corner of the crossing of what became Wellington Street and Waterloo Street, across the road from the present Post Office building, a fine church was erected at a cost of about £10,000 and opened on 15th July 1827. The architect was John Baird. An historical notice dating from 1875 said, "The general effect is that of comfort and elegance". It is recorded that many of the congregation found the change advantageous because the road to Anderston was "very partially formed, and unsuitable in bad weather". It is believed that not one member was lost as a result of the move.

The new church had 1,450 seats, and underneath the building was a crypt for burials, to counter the activities of the resurrectionists. The building had a portico with Ionic pillars, not unlike but smaller than the east front of the Royal Bank building in Royal Exchange Square, which also dates from 1827.

The move accomplished, there continued to grow a thriving congregation, matching the times when, after a period of economic depression and grave public health problems, including cholera and typhoid outbreaks in 1832 and 1837, trade and commerce expanded rapidly. A swelling flow of people into Glasgow began, causing severe housing problems.

THE REV. JOHN MITCHELL, D.D., S.T.P.

Congregational activities likewise expanded, and on 23rd November 1835 the congregation formed itself into a Missionary Society, to identify itself as a missionary agency – a constitutional invention which lasted until 1968 and reflected a remarkable and determined drive in home and foreign mission work.

They continued their work in the Anderston area and in 1845 opened in Bishop Street the first of two schools for poor children sponsored by the Church.

The Dorcas Society was formed to make much-needed clothes for the poor, and a library for the congregation was started.

THE REV. JOHN ROBSON, M.A., D.D.

The custom of quarterly Communions began in 1834, and four years later the simultaneous observation of Communion by the whole congregation. Communion cards instead of the old tokens came in 1853.

In 1840 the Rev. John Robson of Lasswade was inducted as colleague and successor and it is recorded that at his first service he had the temerity to announce a paraphrase – previously forbidden. Dr. Mitchell, without comment, did the same thing at the afternoon service. The use of hymns was not sanctioned by the Session until 1852.

In 1844, a year after the celebration of his Jubilee, Dr. Mitchell died, leaving Mr. Robson as sole minister. The tablet in the front vestibule – moved from the Wellington Street Church – records the congregation's regard for their first minister. In that same year Glasgow University conferred a D.D. on Mr. Robson.

For many years after 1842 the congregational roll was stable at around 1300 members.

Interest in music as a component of worship grew from 1847 when the first choir was started, although it did not last long. The choir was reformed, however, in 1859, and was "closely supervised" by the Session.

In 1847 the reconciliation of the Churches in Scotland continued with the joining of the United Secession and Relief Churches to form the United Presbyterian Church – the "U.P.". Now there were "the Auld Kirk", "the Free Kirk", and "the U.P." – and it was said that the message of the rival bells was:

"I'm saved, I'm saved" – the Auld Kirk

"A' doot it – A' doot it" – the Free Kirk

and "C'lection, C'lection" – the U.P.

In 1847 the congregation, which through its Sabbath School Society was running several Sunday Schools in the neighbourhood and across the river and supported three city missionaries, opened another day school in Cheapside Street. In the same year the system of religious training in the congregation's Sabbath Schools was remodelled, and a regular pattern of Sunday classes began, with advanced classes taught by the minister.

1851 saw the start of the Literary Association for men.

In 1854 came a major development which was to have significant influence on Wellington's activities through the decision to build the Piccadilly Mission at 21 to 25 Piccadilly Street, where most of the Congregation's educational and home mission work was thereafter concentrated. The building was opened on 7th June 1858. The title to the property was taken in name of trustees for the congregation in 1856 and was later transferred to the trustees under the present 1885 constitution. The new mission was only a few steps from the site of the old church in Cheapside Street.

In 1859 the Loch Katrine Waterworks were opened and brought untold benefit to the expanding city. Before that Anderston had no piped water and drew water from wells in the streets.

In 1862 a major extension was started to the west of the church building in Waterloo Street. The old vestry and church officer's house, situated behind the church, were demolished and a new annexe erected which contained a hall to accommodate 400, a session house, minister's room, beadle's residence and committee rooms. In the church itself the pulpit was rebuilt, larger than was then usual and placed lower down over a platform fitted for the use of the Session at Communion services and of parents on the occasion of baptisms. The entrance to the crypt was arched over and now passed under the extended buildings.

Shortly after Dr. Robson's semi-jubilee was celebrated, Dr. James Black of St. Andrews was inducted in 1868 as colleague and successor. In 1872 Dr. Robson died and his memorial tablet is also now in the front vestibule. Dr. Black was in sole charge.

We read at this time of the extending of work with young people, the opening of Penny Banks, and of the Band of Hope to counter the growing abuse of alcohol. The congregation maintained their day school in Piccadilly Street, giving secular and religious education to as many as 400 children. On the Sabbath the hall was used in the forenoon for religious services suitable for the children and young people of the neighbourhood and in the evening for an ordinary Sabbath School.

The Wellington Street U.P. Church was probably the first to produce an enhanced stipend for its ministers. From 1822 they had devoted the afternoon collection wholly to religious and charitable purposes "beyond themselves". In the year to September 1872 they contributed an aggregate of £4,919.12s.10d for congregational purposes and the wider work of the

Church at home and abroad. They maintained four Bible women and four city missionaries, and they had 127 Sabbath School teachers with 1,387 children under their care.

In 1874 a brick church was erected in Lancefield Street to accommodate the increasing work in Cranstonhill, and a new congregation – the "Cranstonhill U.P." – was formed with Wellington's support.

The Congregation by this time contained a representative spread of Glasgow folk and included many well known in the city in industrial, commercial and professional and public life.

It was a time of profound change. The industrial revolution had brought manufacturing resources, and the development of the upper Clyde as a major port brought trade. The city had begun to expand, mainly to the west – out of the smoke from industrial plant and domestic coal fire chimneys carried north-eastwards by the prevailing wind – and in particular over the Kelvin to "the West End".

Meantime, on 12th November 1875, the other congregation derived from the same Anti-Burgher root moved from their church in Montrose Street to their handsome new building in Woodlands Road.

In 1877 the jubilee of the Wellington Street building was duly celebrated.

The Second Move

The Removal Committee found the problem of the crypt in Wellington Street a complex one. Eventually, after much anxious consideration, the congregation approved of the steps to be taken and, with the interests of families and others concerned very much in mind, a Private Act of Parliament was introduced in the House of Lords and having passed through both houses as an unopposed Bill, was passed with the Queen's Assent on 3rd July 1879 (Wellington Street United Presbyterian Church (Glasgow) Act 1879; 42 and 43 Vict. Ch. lxv).

Its preamble outlines the need to provide for the removal and re-interment elsewhere of the remains of persons buried in the crypt, coupled with this text:

> "Whereas, by reason of the changes which have taken place in the city of Glasgow since the erection of the church, which is now surrounded by business premises and is in close proximity to an extensive central railway station, and of the removal to a great extent of the residential population to other parts of the city and suburbs, the congregation may find it necessary or expedient to sell and dispose of the said church, and out of the proceeds of such sale to purchase other land and erect another church more conveniently situated and better suited for the purposes of the said congregation . . ."

Statutory power was thus given to clear the crypt and sell the property; the way was open to build a new church and to borrow money on the security of the property to finance these developments.

Detailed arrangements provided for the removal of the remains of 820 people to the Necropolis in terms of an agreement with the Merchants' House of Glasgow, or elsewhere by private arrangement, and the crypt, after an inspection by the Sheriff, was declared formally cleared on 29th March 1880.

The Removal Committee took professional advice about a new site and their Surveyors' report considered:

1. Four sites south of Sauchiehall Street, two on the east and west sides of Elmbank Street near Bath Street (one of these is now the King's Theatre), one between St. Andrews Halls and North Street (now the Mitchell Library) and one west of Claremont Street between Berkeley Street and Kent Road (now a school).

2. A site north of Sauchiehall Street and east of St. George's Road, another
    west of Cambridge Street and north of Hill Street (now Fleming
    House); several hilly sites on the north side of Sauchiehall Street and
    west of what is now the McLellan Galleries block, and a small site on the
    east side of St. George's Road.

3. Various sites north of Sauchiehall Street and west of St. George's Road;
    others on the west side of St. George's Road and north of Woodlands
    Road, and one in West Cumberland Street, (now Ashley Street);
    another site immediately to the east of St. Silas' Episcopal Church (later
    Woodside Secondary School and now the Woodlands Teachers'
    Centre); and sites south of Great Western Road on the Blythswood
    Estate and at the west end of Sauchiehall Street at Kelvingrove Street.

4. West of the Kelvin. The site of Oakfield House at the east corner of Ann
    Street (now Southpark Avenue) and what was then Woodlands Road
    (now University Avenue) "overlooking the College grounds", and
    other sites in Hillhead.

It is interesting to note that the Presbytery intervened strongly in the
interests of other Churches and was very much against a move to any other
site than west of the Kelvin in the Burgh of Hillhead, and that the Removal
Committee "after much fluctuation of opinion eventually came to the same
conclusion, all but unanimously". It cannot be doubted, with the wisdom of
hindsight, that this decision was wise: all the other sites would have suffered
earlier onset of most of the difficulties which were to assail Wellington at a
later date.

Steps were taken to advertise the Wellington Street site for sale, but the
first responses were few and disappointing and it was soon clear that the
asking price was too high. It was then boldly decided nevertheless to go
ahead and buy a new site with funds made available by members of the
congregation, and to re-advertise the old site at a lower price.

In February 1882, the Removal Committee were at the stage of
choosing one of two sites in Hillhead:

1. The south-east corner of the grounds of Saughfield House on the
    western side of the hill where University Gardens is now; and

2. Oakfield House – the site eventually chosen.

At a Special General Meeting of the Congregation on 28th March 1882,
the Removal Committee was re-appointed with Mr. David Rowan as
Convener and "authorised forthwith to purchase one or other in their
discretion of the above sites, giving preference to the Oakfield House site,
and to procure plans for the erection of a Church, Session House, Hall and

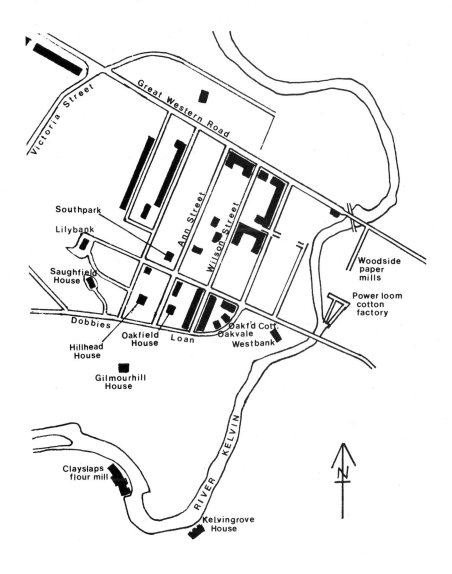

Hillhead Burgh became part of Glasgow in 1891 – when many street names were changed. (*From Ordnance Survey Map in People's Palace, Glasgow 1857–60 approx.*).

other buildings, and cause such Church and buildings to be erected thereon by contract in the usual way, with power to borrow money on the security of the property to cover the cost".

The Oakfield House site was preferred because "it is nearer both to the city and to the foot of the hill, and commands an open space in front". It may well be that this choice did not show the imaginative foresight otherwise the hallmark of the move since the other site lower down on the west side of the hill, while less commanding, would have been more conveniently accessible to the growing residential area to the west and the transport axes which were to develop in Byres Road and Highburgh Road.

By 12th April 1882 the Removal Committee learned that their offer of £4,750 for the Oakfield House site had been accepted, and they decided in principle on a church to accommodate 1,200 (later somewhat reduced) at a cost of between £10,000 and £12,000.

Despite previous indications, there was now some anxious discussion in the Presbytery, the basic trouble being that "Wellington Street Church was one of the strongest and most influential congregations in the U.P. Church". While it had been reported that the congregation had maintained its numbers of loyal members on the promise of a move, and some were prepared to move their homes to the vicinity of the new church, some members of Presbytery thought they were abandoning some of their members and relinquishing good work in the city. Furthermore they were going into an area where within "a relatively small radius" (people were prepared to walk farther in those days!) there were already 11 U.P., 7 Free, 2 Established and 2 Episcopal places of worship, and there was a danger of the congregation disintegrating. Approval of the move was, however, granted.

The Background to the Move

The explosive growth of Glasgow in the nineteenth century was the product of the industrial revolution and the improvement in communications, which together produced rapidly increasing prosperity and a significant confidence characteristic of the Victorian age. Glasgow benefited from its resources in iron, steel, steam power, shipbuilding, railways and engineering, and became "The Second City of the Empire". It is interesting to set Wellington's story against the background of the times, and to recognise how consistent they are. These dates may help to place in context some of the events which resulted from the changes in Glasgow and show the growth of the West End, against which Wellington made its decision to move.

14

1822	A suspension bridge was erected over the Kelvin on the line of what later became Gibson Street.
1834	The first steamship crossed the Atlantic.
1839/40	A high-level bridge was opened over the Kelvin on the line of Great Western Road (the previous bridge was at an angle off South Woodside Road and down near the water level).
1842	The (private) Botanic Gardens were opened.
1842	The first rail connection between Glasgow and Edinburgh.
1844	The Wellington monument erected in Queen Street.
1845	Kirklee Terrace (Windsor Terrace) was erected (the first of the Great Western Road terraces).
1849	Kew Terrace was erected.
1852/53	The Kelvingrove Park was established.
1853	A road bridge was built over the Kelvin on the Woodlands Road line.
1855	Grosvenor Terrace was erected.
1855/58	Ruskin Terrace (St. James Terrace) and Hamilton Park Terrace were erected.
1856	Belgrave Terrace and Granby Terrace (2/28 Hillhead Street) were erected.
1858	Crown Circus was erected – a striking sight on its own on top of the Dowanhill crest with no Byres Road or buildings in between. (The red sandstone period was roughly 1890-1910.)
1858/59	70-80 Oakfield Avenue was erected.
1862	Southpark Terrace was erected.
1862/63	Kelvinside Parish Church built. Lansdowne Church built.
1863	St. Silas Episcopal Church built.
1865	41-53 Oakfield Avenue (by "Greek" Thomson) was erected.
1865/66	Dowanhill Church built.
1866/74	Belhaven Terrace was erected.
1869	Great Western Terrace (by "Greek" Thomson) was erected. Hillhead became a Police Burgh.
1869/70	The Glasgow Tramway and Omnibus Company introduced horse-drawn trams.

1870	Old Queen Margaret Bridge built over the Kelvin, leading to the steps to Wilton Street (It is now demolished).
1870	The University of Glasgow opened on Gilmorehill – first classes held; visited by Queen Victoria.
1870/71	St. Mary's Episcopal Cathedral built.
1872	Horse-drawn trams ran from St. George's Cross along Great Western Road as far as Belhaven Terrace.
1873/77	St. Andrews Halls built (gutted by fire in 1962).
1873	The Kibble Palace was moved from Coulport on Loch Long to the Botanic Gardens.
1874/76	WOODLANDS CHURCH built. (Now the Free Presbyterian Church of Scotland – St. Jude's Congregation.)
1875	Cooper's Store and clock tower appeared on Great Western Road at the Bank Street corner.
1875/77	The Stock Exchange was erected.
1875/76	The Head Post Office erected in George Square.
1875/76	Hillhead Parish Church in Huntly Gardens and Grosvenor Crescent erected.
1875/79	St. Enoch Station and Hotel built.
1876	The Western Baths opened.
1877/79	Kelvinside Academy built (opened 1878).
1878	Failure of the City of Glasgow Bank.
1878	Glasgow Academy moved from Elmbank Street to Kelvinbridge.
1878/80	Athole Gardens built.
1878/80	Queen Street Station built.
1879	Central Station opened.
1879	Westbourne Gardens laid out.
1880	Westbourne Free Church erected.
1883	The Boys' Brigade founded in the Free College Church Mission Hall in North Woodside Road.
1883/85	Hillhead Baptist Church built.
1883/88	The City Chambers built.
1884	WELLINGTON CHURCH.
1884/85	Hillhead High School old building (now Hillhead Primary School) opened 13th April 1885 in Cecil St.

1886	Horse-drawn trams running from Mitchell Street by Charing Cross to Kelvin Bridge.
1886	Hyndland Parish Church built.
1887	Queen Victoria's Jubilee.
1888	The first (of three) International Exhibitions in Kelvingrove Park, visited by Queen Victoria on 22nd August.
1889	Templeton's Carpet Factory (the "Doge's Palace") erected at Glasgow Green.
1890	Hillhead Congregational Church built.
1890	Treron's building in Sauchiehall Street opened.
1890	The Forth (railway) Bridge opened 4th March.
1890/91	New and wider Kelvin Bridge opened 24th September 1891 (old low level bridge removed).
1891	City of Glasgow Act 1891; Hillhead incorporated in Glasgow.
1892/1901	The Art Galleries and Museum built.
1893/94	Belmont Parish Church in Great George Street built (now part of Laurel Bank School).
1894	The Corporation of Glasgow took over the tramway system.
1894	New Gibson Street bridge built over the Kelvin.
1896	Glasgow Subway Railway Company's circle line opened 21st January.
1896	The Caledonian Railway's line under Kelvingrove Park, Great Western Road and Botanic Gardens opened (closed for passengers 1939).
1897/99	The School of Art built (C. Rennie Mackintosh).
1896/1900	University Gardens built.
1900	Kirklee Bridge built over the Kelvin, and 7-23 Kirklee Road built (arguably the finest terrace in the West End, or in all of Glasgow).
1901	The second Exhibition in Kelvingrove Park opened 2nd May 1901.
1901	The first electric trams ran via Eldon Street and Gibson Street to the University. (Originally the terminus was called "Park Road", and then "Gilmorehill" until 1903). A few days later electric trams ran along Byres Road to Botanic Gardens.

| 1903 | Laurel Bank School started in a house called Laurelbank in Glasgow Street (moved to Lilybank Terrace in 1915.) |
| 1904 | Lowther Terrace erected. (No. 8 is now the Church of Scotland Eventide Home, Baxter House). |

This catalogue reveals the remarkable crescendo of development in the city and west end in the second half of the nineteenth century.

It is interesting to note some dates in the history of the University of Glasgow. Founded in 1451, as we are reminded by the Quincentenary Gates opposite the Church, and having moved from Rottenrow to the College site on the High Street, the University moved west before Wellington.

1866	November. Work started on the new buildings on Gilmorehill. (1866/72).
1868	8th October. Foundation stone laid by HRH The Prince of Wales (later Edward VII).
1870/71	First classes held.
1878/84	The Bute and Randolph Halls were being built at the same time as Wellington Church.
1887	Pearce Lodge moved from the Old College and rebuilt at the foot of University Avenue.
1887/88	The tower was built.
1887/95	The original Students' Union built at the top of University Avenue. The openwork spire was added to the tower.
1923/29	The Memorial Chapel and other accommodation enclosed the west side of the quadrangle.
1937	The new Men's Union at the foot of University Avenue opened.
1939	The circular Reading Room was built on the Hillhead House site.
1960	The Stevenson Physical Education building in Oakfield Avenue opened.
1966	The new refectory across Southpark Avenue from Wellington was opened.
1968	The new Library dominated the hill top in Hillhead Street.
1976	The Hunterian Art Gallery, incorporating the Charles Rennie Mackintosh rooms formerly at 78 Southpark Avenue, was opened.

The sort of city in which the move took place is extensively chronicled but it is rewarding to read *Wax Fruit*, the outstanding novel by Guy McCrone which paints so graphic a picture of those very years in the city centre and the west end when Wellington's move took place. It is also instructive to read Professor S. G. Checkland's book *The Upas Tree* about the development of Glasgow from 1875 to 1980. The upas tree of Java was believed to have the power to destroy other growths over a wide radius. Here it is taken as the symbol of the heavy industries which dominated the economy and society of Glasgow for so long and provided the city's spectacular rise and fall. It is fascinating to see how Wellington's life and work moved in step with the economic and social factors illustrated in this book, of which a reviewer said, "It describes what it felt like to be a Glaswegian".

Old maps and the Sasine Register of title deeds show the development of the Hillhead area, which is so happily remembered and illustrated in the delightful *Hillhead Album* (1973) by Henry Brougham Morton.

At the time when the Congregation began in Anderston (1792) the only buildings on the Hillhead slopes were farms. There was a ford at Kelvinbridge. With the construction and later improvement of the bridges over the Kelvin came rapid development as the list of dates shows. We are particularly interested in the three large houses and their grounds which stood on the north side of what is now University Avenue but which at various times was called Dobbie's Loan (as late as 1861, and a continuation of the old track to the west from Cowcaddens) and for a time Woodlands Road.

Saughfield House stood on the sloping ground which became University Gardens and Lilybank Gardens, above the bend in University Avenue, and was one of the sites considered for Wellington's move. Hillhead House stood where the circular University Reading Room is. Many members will remember its brick garden wall across the road from the church, which lasted till 1970.

The third was Oakfield House, the property bought by the Congregation. This was feued out in 1849 as "the house lot of the upper part of the lands of Oakfield, part of the twenty shilling land of old extent of Byres of Partick and Hillhead", and the title deeds describe it as bounded on the west by the centre of Ann Street (Southpark Avenue), on the east by plots on Wilson Street (Oakfield Avenue) and on the south the ground included "the private road from Partick to Glasgow", then 23 feet wide, the boundary being "the mean or mutual wall with the lands of Gilmourhill" (*sic*). The owner was required to pay a contribution for the upkeep of the road to the iron suspension bridge over the Kelvin, and to the bridge money.

19

The University's move to Gilmorehill caused a flurry of development, and in 1872 an agreement was entered into between the Burgh of Hillhead, the University of Glasgow, and the owners of Saughfield, Hillhead House and Oakfield House, about the widening and maintenance of the street now to be called University Avenue, where "public inconvenience was being caused by the narrowness of the said street, and by its not being properly formed, levelled and causewayed". The University gave up land on its north boundary and the proprietors of properties on the north side set back their frontages to give a 60-foot wide street with 10-foot pavements.

The site was bought by the Congregation at Whitsunday 1882 for £4,750, and the title taken in names of individual members in trust, pending the sale of the old church and the removal of the need for bridging finance, and was disponed to the Trustees of the Congregation acting under the new Constitution of 1885; the recording date was 4th July 1889.

The Plans (see endpapers)

A list of architects was chosen, and a Memorandum of particulars on which to base their designs was prepared which stated, "The style not to be Gothic and not to include a tower or steeple, and to be not dis-similar in general character to the present church". It was stated that the site had a rise of about seventeen feet from south to north, and that "a carriage approach to the front entrance is desired, to retire by Ann Street at the north end" (which never happened!). Plans were required by 31st May 1882.

It had been decided to have 1,050 seats, and 350 in the hall, and that the hall must not be under the church, and further, that there must be ample accommodation for an organ and choir. At Wellington Street, while a harmonium was in use in the hall, no instrument was used in the church, so that this was a major innovation.

Early in June, the Removal Committee had sixteen plans before them, and a sub-committee was asked to report. They decided on a short leet of five plans, and after taking further professional advice, the Removal Committee on 22nd June 1882 selected the plan of Mr. T. L. Watson.

Thomas Lennox Watson, L.A., F.R.I.B.A. (1850-1920) received his early architectural training in Glasgow. In London he served as assistant to Alfred Waterhouse, R.A., and worked on several important public buildings in England. After his return to Glasgow he designed many churches, schools, public buildings, country houses – and yacht interiors. He became President of the Glasgow Institute of Architects and President of the Architectural Section of the Royal Philosophical Society of Glasgow and a Governor of the Glasgow and West of Scotland Technical College.

His buildings included the Evening Citizen offices in St. Vincent Place (1889/90), Adelaide Place Baptist Church (1875), the Royal Clyde Yacht Club at Hunter's Quay, and in 1883 our near neighbour Hillhead Baptist Church. He will be best remembered for Wellington, summed up as "Roman Classical, with a Renaissance interior".

The plans were displayed to the Congregation at their Annual Meeting on 4th October 1882, and thereafter schedules went out to tender to the many contractors and trades required. Test bores of the ground had shown a stiff clay bottom over the whole site.

There then followed detailed discussions with the architect, and interesting changes to the original drawing were made at an early stage. The back half of the basement storey (i.e. under the hall) was not in the event excavated or underbuilt as originally intended. Instead, two additional pillars were decided upon for the front portico behind the second and fifth columns. Only the east, or down-hill, half of the basement or crypt below the church was levelled and constituted as an apartment.

One striking feature of the original design was the fact that while the lateral passage on the ground floor entering at the side door and running between the church and the hall existed, the upper passage did not. The upper part of the apse was designed originally as a choir loft, with the organ placed high up. The present church office on the upper floor was to have been the vestry and the pulpit was to have been lower and thrust forward *below* the choir loft, and reached by an angled stair from the rear of the apse. Moreover, there was to have been a large gap between the church and the hall at the upper passage level so that the organ could serve both church and hall as required. A separate keyboard or manual in the hall was also considered.

It is difficult to resist the inference that the committee were so carried away with the excitement of having an organ that they nearly made a serious mistake!

At the old church, when it had been proposed to bring the harmonium into the church to assist the choir in leading the service of praise, the Session (on 5th December 1882) agreed in principle, provided "there was no fear of disturbing the harmony of the Church by this question being agitated at present". They postponed their decision and decided to consult the congregation about an organ for the new church. Voting papers were issued, and 388 out of 406 said "Yes".

The Removal Committee had accordingly set up an Organ Sub-Committee to work on a first budget of £1,000. Advice was taken and four different specifications devised (identified as Alpha, Beta, Gamma and Delta), and tenders were invited from organ builders, who at first were to

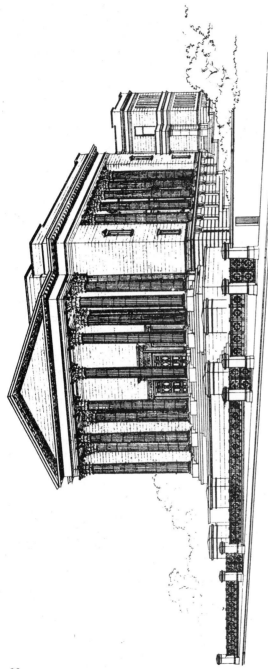

Buildings, University Avenue, for
WELLINGTON STREET UNITED PRESBYTERIAN CHURCH
GLASGOW 1st December 1882.

J. J. Watson
Architect

22

quote both with and without a separate keyboard in the hall. The Organ Sub-Committee however were strongly advised that this would increase the cost of building, repairing and tuning the organ, and alternative proposals were then prepared, but still showing the opening between the church and the hall. Applicants were invited to comment on the four alternative specifications and on the difficulties (including draughts) which might result from this opening. Shortly afterwards, on further advice from a consultant and from the organ builders, this layout too was abandoned and the present arrangement adopted. The vestry was relocated on the ground floor and the church sealed off from the hall with the upper corridor passing between. The pulpit was raised and had steps up on both sides. The whole space was left for the organ and the choir placed on a platform on floor level, forward of the organ case and pulpit.

Forster & Andrews of Hull were the successful builders, and it was decided to have three manuals; the "Gamma" specification was preferred, and it was found possible to bring the cost within the final budget of £1200.

The organ originally had an engine worked by water pressure. This soon gave trouble and had to be extensively overhauled.

There were considerable problems of bridging finance while the Wellington Street site remained unsold, but loans from members were obtained on the security of the old building.

There were anxious moments when the large stones for the front pillars were delayed, and over a problem of completing the roof while the contractors' large crane was still in use, but the architect dealt with these matters. By December 1883 the mason work was done and the roof was well advanced.

Preparations were meantime going ahead for financing the running of the new church and reviewing the financial system in Wellington as a whole: it was, however, decided to continue raising money for Wellington and Home Missions by collections and for Foreign Missions through visiting collectors. The seat rents to be payable in the new church (in the pre-Weekly Freewill Offering days the traditional method of ensuring payment of the stipend and other standing charges) were carefully considered to produce £800 approximately. 915 sittings were taken up immediately, and there was difficulty in meeting all the requests.

At a Special Meeting of the Congregation the appointment of an organist was approved and a committee was elected to seek candidates. The short leet played in Claremont Church on 14th July 1884 and Mr. Fred Turner, who was blind, was appointed. He was to bring the utmost distinction to his work and gloriously enhanced the worship of the congregation, and he was still at the organ stool fifty years later.

Only after several attempts to sell the old church at reducing asking prices was an offer of £12,000 received in August 1884, after a possible sale to the Caledonian Railway Company fell through. At this point it was decided to put a leaflet in the pews revealing the figures for the sale and purchase, and urging a liberal collection on the opening Sunday.

The closing services at Wellington Street were on Sunday 5th October 1884 at 11 a.m., Rev. George Jeffrey, D.D. and 2 p.m., Rev. James Black, D.D.

The old church became a suite for functions called "The Waterloo Rooms"; later the Alhambra Theatre was erected on the site and after its closing and demolition, an office block.

The Congregation decided that its new name was "Wellington United Presbyterian Church" and "Wellington" it has been known as ever since.

MR. FRED TURNER

The Opening of the New Church, 1884

The new church buildings were opened on Saturday 11th October 1884 at 3 p.m. by the Rev. John Cairns, D.D., LL.D., Principal of the University of Glasgow. Tickets for the ceremony were issued by the elders. The text was Isaiah 55, verse 8: "For my thoughts are not your thoughts, neither are your ways my ways, saith the Lord."

Three services were conducted on Sunday 12th October 1884.

Morning at 11 o'clock. Preacher: Rev. Professor Calderwood, LL.D.

His text was Ephesians 2: 22, "(Jesus Christ himself being the chief cornerstone) In whom ye also are builded together for an habitation of God through the Spirit."

Afternoon at 2 o'clock. Preacher: Rev. James Black, D.D.

His text was 2 Chronicles 6: 18, "But will God in very deed dwell with men on the earth? behold, heaven and the heaven of heavens cannot contain thee; how much less this house which I have built!"

Evening at 6.30. Preacher: Rev. John M. Sloan, M.A. (of Free Anderston Church).

His text was Revelation 21: 22, "And I saw no temple therein: for the Lord God Almighty and the Lamb are the temple of it."

The famous collection, recorded without comment in our Collection Book as taken at these services, was £11,171.13s.2¾d. (*sic*), later made up to £11,277.

It is noted elsewhere that the widow of Dr. John Robson, the second minister, who had been assisted by the Congregation after his death in 1872, and her circumstances being changed, put the whole sum she had received in the plate that day.

On Monday 13th October, Dr. E. Hopkins of the Temple Church, London, who had been invited formally to take over the organ from the builders, gave an organ recital with Mr. Turner in aid of the Royal College of the Blind.

"The Glasgow Herald" (price one penny in those days) tells us that at the time of the opening – in the year when all men got the vote in parliamentary and local government elections, and when the steam turbine was invented – Mr. D'Oyley (*sic*) Carte's Opera Company were opening in "Iolanthe" at the Royalty Theatre (later the YMCA's Lyric Theatre) on

Monday 6th October, a day of dense fog in Glasgow; the Caledonian Railway express to London took 10 hours with a 25-minute stop at Preston for dinner. The Clyde was alive with steamer services, and the Ben Nevis Observatory was providing daily weather reports.

The following article appeared on Saturday 11th October:

Wellington U.P. Church

The spacious edifice just completed for the congregation hitherto worshipping in Wellington Street U.P. Church is to be formally opened today by the Rev. Principal Cairns, D.D. The new church forms one of the most important of recent additions to the ecclesiastical architecture of Scotland, and is in every way worthy of the fine site it occupies at the corner of Ann Street, Hillhead, immediately to the north of the Glasgow University. The principal front of the church consists of a portico of ten fluted Corinthian columns, approached by an open flight of steps from University Avenue. From the portico three large outer doorways lead into the vestibule, and from the vestibule four doors open into the area floor of the church, while stairs on each side lead to the galleries. At the north end of the church another two gallery stairs are provided, and there is a spacious corridor on each floor. The church itself is about 90 x 60 x 47 feet high inside. Its general form is rectangular in plan, with a gallery recess at the south end and an organ recess at the north, the latter being covered by a half dome, richly moulded and decorated. The ceiling of the church consists of three arched or vaulted spans, carried on two longitudinal beams stretching from end to end of the church and without pillars. The sides of the ceiling are coved and groined, and the whole is enriched with arched ribs and panels. The construction of the roof is of a quite novel character, consisting of two malleable iron lattice girders, about 80 feet long and over 7 feet deep, stretching from one end of the church to the other. Between these two girders the middle arch of the ceiling rises, and between the walls and the girders the side arches spring, and the ceiling is thus supported entirely on the girders and side walls. The roof principals and purlins are also of malleable iron. The church is provided with side and end galleries, and seats 1050 persons, with a liberal amount of space to each. The width of exits is nearly 50 per cent. in excess of the minimum rule laid down by authorities on this subject, and all the doors open outwards as well as inwards. The acoustic qualities of the church have been the subject of careful study, and all that experience could suggest has been done to make the undertaking successful in this respect. The proportions of the building, form of ceiling, the setting out of seats, and the materials used throughout the interior have all been considered with regard to their influence on sound. To the north of the church are situated the hall, 50 by 35, with an end gallery; the library, 35 by 21; and session-house, vestry, ladies' room, and numerous class-rooms, together with a church officer's house. The total length of the building, including the outside stair, is about 200 feet, and its width at the north end is 100 feet. The height of the apex of the pediment above University Avenue is about 75 feet. The columns of the portico and side walls, of which there are 20, are 35 feet high and 3 feet 6 inches diameter. The total cost of the building – exclusive, however, of the cost of the site, organ, furniture, etc. – is £15,000. The stone used is from Overwood Quarry.

The following are some of the leading contractors for the work:–

Masons, Messrs. James Watson & Son; wrights, Messrs. Allan & Baxter; slater, Mr. William McEwen; plumbers, Messrs. Wallace & Connell; plasterer, Mr. R. A. McGilvray; heating engineers, Messrs. J. Combe & Sons; painters, Messrs. A. & J. Scott; glaziers, Messrs. William Meikle & Sons and Messrs. W. & J. J. Kier; gasfitters, Messrs. D. & G. Graham and Messrs. R. Laidlaw & Son; ventilating, Messrs. J. G. Carrick & Co.; marble mosaic pavements, Messrs. Walker & Emley; wrought-iron railing and gates, Mr. R. A. Stoffert. In working out the iron girders of the roof the architect consulted with Messrs. Wharrie, Colledge & Brand, civil engineers; and this contract was carried out by Messrs. Arrol, of Germiston Ironworks. The organ has been built by Messrs. Forster & Andrews of Hull. Mr. T. L. Watson, F.R.I.B.A., is the architect.

At the Annual Meeting on 6th October 1885 the Managers formally took charge of the new building from the Removal Committee and sub-committees. The total cost had been £29,702.

Receipts		Payments	
Collection	11,277	Site, new church and furnishings	26,468
Other contributions	425	Expenses of the move including clearing of crypt at Wellington Street	3,234
Sale of old site	12,000		
Balance (which was cleared by 2nd April 1889)	6,000		
	£29,702		£29,702

The organ cost £1,126 and was paid for from a special organ fund which was quickly raised after the decision to have an organ for the first time.

The Story from 1884

Since our thoughts in 1984 are of one hundred years in our present building, there follows an account of the building itself, and thereafter a separate diary of congregational matters.

1. THE CHURCH BUILDINGS, 1884-1984
A diary of events, developments and changes

1885   Many minor improvements and additions were made,including pulpit lights; furniture for the choir platform and hall platform (some will remember the moveable rostra, and the hard carpeting which lasted for an incredible number of years); lamps and rails for the front steps; a lamp at the side door porch. Ten metal capitals were added to the tops of the metal columns supporting the gallery. Some of the stonework was treated with oil where it was flaking.

1889   The choir platform was altered to permit of the choir facing the congregation. There was no communion table in the much less spacious area then available.

1890   The building was of course gas-lit and this produced much heat. The necessary openings in the church roof are obvious. Many have observed all over the buildings the circular wooden plaques on the walls betraying the original positions of the gas brackets. There was trouble with ventilation and draughts. Have you noticed the handles at the air ducts by the church

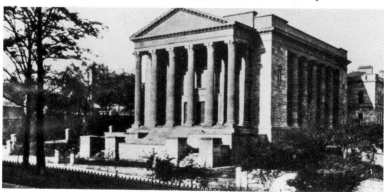

WELLINGTON CHURCH, 1884

28

windows? These look like cleats, but in fact rotate shutters which admitted fresh air from the basement. The corner seats and the choir area were particularly affected.

1895 A member had a personal speaking tube installed from the pulpit to his seat! The Church Officer had recurring difficulties with the palm trees in tubs which then graced the choir stalls and pulpit steps.

1896 Notice boards were placed in the grounds for the first time.

1902 A decision to hold evening services instead of afternoon services on Sundays convinced the Managers that improvements to the lighting were desirable. Their minutes record on 23rd September, "In view of the Sabbath evening services, it was considered whether the electric light (*sic*) should not be introduced". The congregation approved on 7th October and by 28th December this major change was completed. The original flat ring light fittings with their gas jets and globes and pilot lights were removed and new electroliers hung consisting of metal bowls – originally with no lining or interior lights – carrying hanging lamps below; (two large ones in the centre and three smaller ones on each side above the side balconies, with one in the back gallery). These were designed by the Bromsgrove Guild of Applied Arts. These handsome lamp fittings were based on an early Christian design described as Coptic polycandelons, and are understood to have been copies of lamps which hung in the Cathedral of St. Sophia in Constantinople. The symbols on the bowls include:

 A Ω, *Alpha* and *Omega*, the first and last letters of the Greek alphabet (Revelation 1, verse 8).

 Xp the Greek letters for Ch and r, the beginning of the word *Christos* or Christ.

 The interpretation of this is less clear, but an expert suggests:–

θ in the centre is the Greek letter for Th, *theta*, first letter of *Theos* or God.

Ϸ at the top is thought to be Xp, again as above,

A and ω (another form of Ω) are the *Alpha* and *Omega*, as above.

E is the first letter of the Greek word *EUAGGALION* or evangel – the gospel (or it may be for Emmanuel).

THE NEW LIGHTS TODAY

1902	At the same time, terrazzo paving was installed to replace unsatisfactory slabs on the front exterior landing, and the top portions of the upper church windows were made to open.
1903	On 14th May a useful profit was made by erecting stands and seating to view the procession of King Edward VII and Queen Alexandra past the Church. They later laid the foundation stone of the Royal Technical College. The money was used to plant (on 17th December) four trees at the side of the Church – 1. Spruce. 2. Elm. 3. Red chestnut. 4. Service.
1908	Fittings were attached to the bookboards in the pews to receive the individual communion cups.
1910	May. Black and purple drapes were obtained for the pulpit for King Edward VII's funeral.
1911/12	The organ blower and its engine were overhauled, and the "noisy mechanism" repaired. The Church was closed from March to September for repainting.
1913	Further additions and improvements were made to the organ.
1914	The memorial tablet to Dr. James Black was erected in the front vestibule.

30

1914/19	The First World War.
1921	On Sunday 17th April the 1914-1919 War Memorial was dedicated. It carries 54 names. A suggestion that it be sited in the front vestibule was dropped, and the oak memorial and lettering, designed by Sir John James Burnet, LL.D., R.S.A., A.R.A., was mounted on the organ case. The carved wreath enclosing the dove returning with a leaf – emblem of the old United Presbyterian Church – was part of the design.
1924/26	Urgent repairs were done to the fabric, the lighting and the organ, and the Church was closed in July and August 1926 for painting.
1928	Access by the side door was improved by making a second door out of a window and extending the stone porch. The hall was redecorated.
1930	On 19th October the memorial tablet to Dr. Morrison was unveiled in the front vestibule.
1931	The congregation received a gift of chairs to replace pews and forms in the library and the hall.
1934	The 50th anniversary of the present church buildings. This milestone was marked by major improvements to the Church interior.

Two pews were removed from the centre front of the area and the choir platform extended forward. On it was installed the communion table with its top of marble from Iona, together with the three chairs, a new screen for the organist's seat and console – then below the pulpit – and new choir stalls, in padouk wood, designed by Whytock & Reid. Additional space was provided by removing the angled stairs leading up to the pulpit on each side and substituting a single straight stair up to its east side, in keeping with the new surroundings.

The common cup and bread platter in silver, two brass vases and a reading desk and Bible for the table, the alms dish in brass, and the cloth of fine linen completed the gifts.

The consulting architect was Sir. D. Y. Cameron. The vessels were designed by Edward Spencer.

All this effected a striking alteration in the appearance of the Church. In his sermon at the Service of Dedication on Sunday 7th October Mr. Jarvis, who was only sad that the windows had not been improved – that had to wait until 1962 – said, "beauty is no longer suspect as savouring of the devil".

Acousticons were installed to help the deaf.

1934	At the Jubilee Social on Tuesday 9th October, the Very Rev. Dr. John White in his address recalled the opening in 1884 when he had been struck by three factors for which Wellington remained famous – its ministers, its buildings, and its liberality.
1935/36	The process of improvement continued, with the help of a generous gift from an old member. The two large lanterns over the centre of the area had always had windlasses in the loft for lowering them for cleaning and servicing; windlasses were now fitted to the other seven. The old exposed light bulbs below the bowls which caused glare were replaced by bulbs in cup-type metal shades.
	The fine new baptismal font was provided.
	A new self-firing central heating boiler was installed with thermostatic controls, and extra radiators were fitted in some of the rooms and corridors.
	The doors leading into the church, previously covered in red cloth, were panelled in African walnut and the bookboard round the front balcony similarly treated, in keeping with the communion table and chairs and choir stalls.
1938	This was the year when the Fabric Fund was started and a special collection was taken on Foundation or Anniversary Sunday – fixed as the first Sunday in October, before the October Communion service on the second Sunday.
	The stone platforms at the side of the front steps were polished and protected.
1939/45	The years of the Second World War. The whole country was required to show no lights at night which might assist enemy aircraft. Arrangements were made to black out the premises – a considerable problem. Sandbags were filled and placed in the crypt to make an air raid shelter, and firefighting and first aid equipment and emergency lighting appliances obtained.
1941/42	The church hall was scheduled as a temporary shelter for war refugees and a contingency emergency rest camp.
1943	Improvements were made to the Acousticon installation.
1948	On the last Sunday in October, two additional War Memorial tablets with 21 names of the fallen in the 1939-45 war were dedicated.
	An ambitious plan to relocate the organ in the back gallery and open up the apse as a main feature to contain both War Memorials was dropped.
1950	Long overdue repairs were carried out to the fabric and the organ,

and the church was closed in August and September while painting was done. The organ was partly rebuilt, and improved by
lifting the central pipe feature and installing the two grills, on
either side of the dove, to allow a better emission of sound. Later,
in 1953, a semi-circular screen on a false cornice was fitted in the
apse with a floodlight, to conceal the obtrusive tuba pipe.

In the hall the Woman's Guild and the Missionary Committee
took the initiative to replace the old dais and its fittings by a new
stage with curtains and lighting, and a door was slapped
through to allow access into the corner of the hall from what was
then a classroom or committee room, formerly "Room 2".

1951 New ventilators were fitted to the church roof, and hymn
boards were brought into use for the first time.

Proposals for improvements in the crypt were postponed
because a building licence could not be obtained owing to post-
war restrictions on supply of materials.

A Christmas Tree was erected on the front steps landing in a
fitting specially made to hold the tree or a flagpole, so that, as
Dr. Jarvis said, "Christmas could be claimed for the Church".
(For over fifty years, the Syme family have provided the Christmas tree in the choir stalls during Advent and Christmas).

1952 The words "CHURCH OF SCOTLAND – WELLINGTON"
were cut on the podium and gilded. A new front notice board of
better design was erected and a floodlight installed behind it.

1953 There was increasing anxiety at this time about the impact of
the Town and Country Planning (Scotland) Acts and the effect
on Wellington of the zoning of the whole area between
University Avenue and Great George Street on both sides of the
hill as predominantly for University use and development,
coupled with persistent rumours of stopping through traffic in
University Avenue, and cutting off access from the north.
Assurances were received from the planning authority on 19th
May 1974 that the local authority did not propose to remove
existing churches from areas zoned for industrial and open
space uses – no mention was made of the University zone – and
that the Secretary of State felt sure that when carrying out their
road proposals, the local authority would pay particular
attention to the possible effect on churches of historic or
architectural value.

This was the year of the coronation of HRH Queen Elizabeth II,
and the new flagpole carried one of the countless flags which
bedecked the city.

| 1953 | On Saturday 14th March the No. 1 District, Northern Division of the Girl Guides Association planted a flowering cherry tree in the church grounds to mark the Coronation. |

Miss Jessie M. Stewart, who died in 1950, had left a substantial bequest of one-half of the residue of her estate to Wellington, and further capital funds became available from the sale in 1949 of Stobcross House, the Church's Mission Hall in Anderston. Plans were prepared to provide a major extension to the hall accommodation and to improve the church officer's house, and were discussed at a Special Meeting on 31st March. The dingy compartment between the hall and the library, partly under the hall gallery, was reconstructed to provide a kitchenette or servery with hatches on both sides, and equipped for catering. Urgent repairs were done to the cornices of the main building. The central heating plant had an overhaul.

The plans for the extension had to conform to planning requirements to fit in with the original buildings and, because of the exposure of the site, this had to be faced with stone. It was designed to contain an upper hall, named the Allan Hall in memory of the benefactor of Stobcross, and two classrooms beneath, named the Stewart Rooms in memory of Miss Jessie M. Stewart. The old No. 2 room was opened through to the extension as an access passage. New and improved toilet accommodation was included. A great improvement in the church officer's house was made by enlarging some of the apartments and providing an internal access stair leading direct to a new side door into the church garden.

At this time there was increasing concern to equip Wellington to serve the University of whose community we were clearly now part, and with a view to further extension should the need arise, the west wall of the Allan Hall includes a beam at floor level so that a further hall could be built and the Allan Hall would become its platform or stage.

The former ladies' room off the upper corridor was converted for use as the Church Office.

This complex operation was under the care of Mr. Ernest D. Webster, the Vice-Preses, as convener of the Managers' Building Committee.

| 1954 | On 21st March the beautiful new lectern was dedicated and a Coronation Bible provided, made possible by Miss Edgar's legacy. |

34

| 1955 | The major extension works were now under way and cost around £11,000. The architect was Alexander Wright, who presented three chairs for the new Allan Hall. |
| 1956 | On Saturday 20th October at 3 p.m. the Allan Hall and Stewart Rooms were dedicated. These greatly improved the amount and flexibility of accommodation at Wellington, and enhanced the work of the Sunday School in particular. |

The Order of Proceedings for the opening and dedication ceremony recorded: "The Congregation of Wellington gave approval to the proposals of its Board of Managers and Missionary Society to use the funds from the sale of the Mission in Anderston and Miss Jessie M. Stewart's legacy to carry out major developments in the buildings to enable Wellington to develop its work in the district and in the University community".

In the same year the room beside the Session House was transformed into a comfortable place for meetings and named "The Guild Room". The ladies of the Congregation made a considerable contribution towards the provision of furnishings for the new accommodation.

200 stacking chairs were brought into use in the hall and library, finally replacing the old benches and pews.

During the year, there was an indecisive plebiscite about a sound reinforcement system to improve the Church acoustics.

| 1959 | A second alms dish, hand-beaten in brass, made by an African boy in Edgerley Memorial School, Duke Town, Old Calabar, Nigeria, established by Mary Slessor, was gifted by an elder, Mr. D. D. R. White. Sadly, this was stolen from the Church many years later following a house-breaking. |
| 1960 | The ventilation, lighting and decoration of the Session House were improved. Old sacking which had blocked off the ceiling vents from the days of gas lighting was discovered! 25 new chairs were provided from the balance of Miss Edgar's legacy. |

On 22nd March a Special Meeting of the Congregation faced up to the need for urgent repairs to the outside stonework, and the redecoration of the interior of the church. The building duly disappeared behind scaffolding in the summer months while the outside work was done.

| 1961 | On the initiative of the Missionary Committee, a Special Meeting on 17th May put in hand a plan to refurbish the crypt and bring it into use for regular congregational purposes, and in particular to make provision in an informal setting for activities involving the University. |

1961	The crypt – previously a dusty cellar with a black asphalt floor and dingy walls – was transformed with a lowered ceiling, new lighting and heating, catering facilities and attractive furnishings. The work, including the simple but impressive Cross feature, was designed by Mr. Geoffrey Jarvis and dedicated on Sunday 12th November 1961.

This development signalled a recovery of confidence about Wellington's role, and had a significant effect in the years ahead.

1962 The Church was closed from July to September for a major overhaul of the interior and, as usual at these times, we enjoyed the hospitality of the Bute Hall in the University for our services. In particular the old etched and yellowing coloured glass windows, very much like those in the City Hall, which had so reduced the natural light in the Church were replaced by fine translucent white glass windows with blue lining. At last the improvement which Sir D. Y. Cameron had wanted in 1934 came about. Further pews were removed from the front of the area to provide better access to the choir platform, which was carpeted in blue, although members missed the old "burning bush" rug which lay on the wooden platform. The biggest change came from the stripping of the old dark-stained and varnished pews which were lightened to an oak colour and treated with polyurethane paint. The two grills in the organ case front were replaced by a new design more in keeping with the church interior. (If you want to see one of the original grills, look at the gate at the foot of the internal stair to the Church Officer's house).

The overhead lanterns were cleaned and greatly improved by interior lighting of the bowls to reveal clearly the cut-out symbols and at the same time to illuminate the handsome roof, and new shades of copper colour were provided for the hanging lamps below the bowls.

The roof was regilded and the roof and walls repainted to complete the overhaul, and the combined effect, by daylight and by night, was remarkable. Mr. Jack R. Notman, A.R.I.B.A., designed and supervised these works.

The hall was redecorated at the same time.

It is interesting to note that St. Andrew's Halls were tragically gutted by fire in October 1962, and Wellington was considered as an emergency concert hall for several events, including the annual performance of "The Messiah".

1963	The central heating boiler was converted from coal to oil burning.
1964	The James Taylor bequest made possible the acquisition of new blue cushions and seat covers for the pews and choir stalls, and completed the matching colours of the enhanced interior.
1965	The memorial to Dr. Jarvis – designed by Mr. Jack R. Notman – in the form of a table and plaque in the front vestibule was dedicated on 30th May.
1966	In August there was an emergency repair to the front steps, where a serious defect was discovered.
1968	The hurricane in January, which caused havoc in Glasgow, damaged the roof but despite its intensity, and the exposure of the site, no serious harm was caused.
1970	A new sound reinforcement system was at last installed in the Church but it was not entirely satisfactory in use.
1973	The lighting in the lanterns was further improved with new and much more efficient bulbs.

The deaf aid provision was extended by the unobtrusive fitting of an induction loop round the gallery frontage to transmit to individual deaf aid sets.

Outside floodlighting was installed and switched on for the Annual Meeting of the Congregation on 27th November.

1974	This was the year of the union with Woodlands congregation, recorded later.

The Church Hall was refurbished and named "The Woodlands Hall" and a blown-up photograph of Woodlands Church displayed. The old obscure glass was removed from the windows and clear glass fitted, new and greatly improved light fittings were installed, and a new floor covering laid. On Tuesday 1st October new and better floodlights were placed outside, and 90 members of the Congregation climbed the University tower to see the effect.

1975	The Woodlands Church War Memorial Tablets (carrying 32 names from the 1914-1918 war and 8 names from the 1939-1945 war), were re-erected in the passage opposite the entrance to the Woodlands Hall, and the Garden of Remembrance from Woodlands was reconstituted and dedicated at the north end of the church garden. A plaque reads,

"Garden of Repose. After cremation the ashes
of those who have passed on rest in this place".

1975	Repairs were done to the steps, guttering and slates. The very large Welsh slates are an unseen feature of the church roof.
1976/77	The Congregation faced up to problems about the fabric, which was not improving with age, and the organ, which was becoming unreliable. Early in 1974 the Managers had asked the organist, Mr. George Wilson, for a report on the organ's condition, and this is partly reproduced elsewhere.

The Session and Managers issued a comprehensive paper to all members and called a Special Meeting of the Congregation on 29th June 1975. The congregation learned how they had kept the matter of the fabric under review, with expert reports taken in 1965, 1967 and 1971 from architects (including Mr. Geoffrey Jarvis), the Historic Buildings Council and the Planning Department (Conservation Section) of the Corporation of Glasgow. The acquisition of funds arising from the union with Woodlands and the sale of that church, together with the sale of the Wellington assistant minister's manse at 127 Hyndland Road and the availability of grant aid, now made it possible to contemplate much needed renovation work on the stonework, including the columns, the cornices and pediment, and the roof. The paper set out very fully the recurring problem of whether to invest more money in the buildings – on the "stitch in time" basis – or to expend the money on activities within Wellington or in the wider work of the Church.

At the meeting on 29th June it was agreed "that subject to the City of Glasgow District Council or other bodies making available a grant of 50% for the repair and renovation of the Wellington Church buildings, the Trustees and Managers instruct and have carried out the proposed external repairs and renovation and allied works, always provided the cost to Wellington shall not exceed £35,000".

There followed a delay due to the commercial failure of the original contractors involved, and it was not until May 1976 that the grant applications were before the District Council.

Meantime, during the latter part of 1975, the Managers were faced with increasing urgency about the condition of the organ, and a special Organ Committee, with Mr. George McPhee, organist of Paisley Abbey as adviser, recommended rebuilding at a cost of about £24,000, with electric action to replace the rapidly deteriorating pneumatic action, and new bellows since the existing leathers had virtually perished. In particular, and because these changes would make it possible, they recommended that the console should be placed elsewhere than immediately below the pulpit, from which position the organist could not conduct the choir and where the organ sound went over the organist's head. It was evident from the report that if nothing were done, the organ might continue playable for another two or three years but could collapse before that.

The Congregation did not have the funds to undertake both the fabric and the organ works. The Managers, after anxious review of all the consequences, and in the light of uncertainty about grant aid for the building, recommended to the Congregation that the organ work be undertaken, and about £6000 spent on essential repairs only to the steps, gutters and slating, and professional fees. At a Special Meeting on 20th June 1976 this was agreed, and on 28th November, so was the interesting proposal to remove the console to the east side gallery. Other possible situations in the front area or east transept had been rejected for structural or practical reasons.

The reconstruction of the organ allowed the removal of the screen which had concealed the full view of the top of the apse, and resulted in more space and a simplified pulpit structure behind the communion table and chairs.

1977   A new notice-board was erected at the front of the Church.

With the help of "Community Industry" internal repainting of the church rooms, including the library and the kitchen, staircases and corridors was carried out.

1980   The Woman's Guild marked its jubilee by commissioning from the Embroiderers' Guild tapestry cushions for the three chairs at the communion table. The minister's chair in the centre has a design matching the Maltese Cross on the table front, while the other two cushions pick up the design of the side galleries.

- - - - - - - - - - - - - -

A reviewer of a recent book describes it as having a major flaw – a failure to distinguish between the trivial and therefore potentially tedious, and the truly significant. What is significant is that we have arrived at 1984 with a magnificent building which successive Boards of Managers and an ever-changing and now markedly diminished Congregation has prayerfully done their best to sustain, improve and pass on. It is an aggregate of minor and major actions which together reflect the concern of the Congregation for their heritage over these hundred years. The Church was built to the glory of God and to provide a place wherein the Congregation might worship God and seek their own communion and inspiration, and which might stand proudly proclaiming, as Church buildings throughout the land do, that God is in His heaven and that our gratitude calls for our offering Him the best we can do. Most importantly of all, the church was intended to form the base from which would spring compassion and service to others specifically in the home and overseas mission fields, and the encouragement and support of the congregation through Christian fellowship.

2. THE CONGREGATION

A diary of events, developments and changes in the life and work of Wellington

There is no possibility that a book of this size could encompass the story of the congregational activities during the hundred years in the present church in a way which would in any way reflect the quality and quantity of individual and corporate activity which evolved as their expression of their duty to love and serve God and to love and serve their neighbours.

The available records by way of minute books, reports, year books, literature, leaflets and souvenirs, personal collections and numerous other sources, together with outside information from public records, have been found to be incomplete in the sense of both missing items and periods of time. There was a further difficulty with records which were meaningful to contemporaries, but often unhelpful to a reader many years later. The story is therefore incomplete.

While an attempt has been made to record a summary of events in this booklet, it would surely be wrong to appraise them. The deep regret is that all the Wellington folk known to have given sustained service to Wellington and its Missions cannot be named here for reasons of space and that hurt may be caused by the mention of some and the omission of others.

It is hoped, however, that the information which follows will awaken memories for many, and illustrate the ways in which the congregation sought to serve the Church by adapting itself to the changing circumstances of the years.

For everyone mentioned by name because of their special position in some context, there are countless others not named who gave valuable service, some in the intensive and inspiring way of leaders but many more whose loyal support though less prominent was none the less vital.

Throughout the years, those whose privilege it was and is to belong to Wellington have known it as a friendly Church. Family worship is an unshaken tradition and Christian fellowship a living reality. Here the opportunity to serve the Church and its neighbours, in the sense Jesus illustrated so vividly when he was asked, "Who is my neighbour?", is always open. The result depends not on the cherished tradition of the past but on what those who are now our members are able and willing to offer as their personal response.

1884–1945

1885 Arising from the move to the new church in 1884, the last Constitution of the Congregation dating from 1828 was superseded by a new Constitution approved by the congregation on 27th May and confirmed on 15th June. It was approved by the Presbytery of Glasgow North on 8th September, signed on 11th September, and registered for preservation in the Sheriff Court Books of Lanarkshire on 12th October 1885.

It followed the United Presbyterian pattern of constitution, providing for Trustees and Managers, being the same sixteen people but with distinct functions. The Trustees are charged with the holding of the congregation's ground, buildings and funds, while the rules for the Managers cover the transacting of the secular or business affairs of the congregation. The Session reserves the right to watch over the whole interest of the congregation and to interpose whenever in its opinion the welfare of the congregation calls upon it to do so, by convening meetings of the congregation or in other ways. This Constitution with only minor changes in details continues today, and the fact that Woodlands Church was also a United Presbyterian congregation with a parallel constitution greatly facilitated the union in 1974.

1886 In November there was a move to have organ voluntaries before and after the services, much desired by the organist, Mr. Turner. The Session said "No" to "after" and cautiously tested the feelings of the congregation, but their vote was inconclusive.

1888 In March it was noted that there was still a balance of £6,000 outstanding on the account for the new church. Mr. Alexander Allan took the initiative to have it cleared: £4,000 was raised by May; the rest was paid off by April 1889.

1889 In this year there is the first mention of Assistant Ministers as a help in training probationers, and the first mention of a wedding ceremony conducted in the church itself.

1890 Mr. Turner, the organist, got his way and the congregation approved of, and enjoyed, organ voluntaries.

1891 The Missionary Society adopted a new Constitution.

THE REV. JAMES BLACK, D.D.

1892/93   On Monday 13th March the congregation met to celebrate the congregation's centenary and Dr. Black's semi-jubilee. At this time the membership was 949.

On Thursday 16th March a choir of 46 (19 sopranos, 8 altos, 9 tenors and 10 basses) performed Mendelssohn's "Elijah".

At the services on Sunday 19th March Dr. Black spoke of the wish "to deepen our feelings of thankfulness and of attachment to the congregation, and intensify our resolution to perpetuate and increase whatever has been good in our congregational life".

1894   Dr. Black withdrew as Senior Minister.

1894/99   The short ministry of Dr. Forrest, recognised as a great scholar, after which Dr. Black resumed in full charge.

1898   The Session approved the introduction of the new Church Hymnary.

1899	The introduction of salaried choir leaders caused controversy. A plebiscite was taken and showed a majority in favour. The move was approved by the Congregation at a meeting on 4th December.
1900	October 4th. The Union of the United Presbyterian and Free Churches to form the United Free Church.
1902	The Rev. George H. Morrison was inducted as minister on 13th May. During his ministry the Congregation increased from 980 to 1,868 leading to the celebrated queues of a Sunday evening in University Avenue. When he was at the height of his powers his preaching filled the church to overflowing with members and visitors.
1904/5	The records show a membership of 1,114, with 20 elders, 19 Sunday School teachers and 163 on their roll, a Choir of 68; there was a Band of Hope, a (mixed) Literary Association of 126; a Christian Endeavour Society, a Dorcas Society, and an active Congregational Library.

THE REV. DAVID W. FORREST, D.D.

THE REV. GEORGE H. MORRISON, M.A., D.D.

1905 (and again in 1921) Proposals to run tramcars over University Avenue came to nothing.

1906   The Girls' Auxiliary started in Wellington.

1907   A choir of 106 performed Handel's "Messiah".

1908   A choir of 117 performed Bach's "St. Matthew Passion".

1909   On 28th October, Mr. Turner received a presentation on his semi-jubilee as organist.

1911   On 21st November there was a reunion and social to mark the diamond jubilee of the Literary Association.

1913	Dr. James Black died on 6th October.
	The Girls' Auxiliary in Wellington now had 200 members.
1914/19	The First World War.
1915/16	A Belgian Relief Committee, which continued until 1919, began to care for 65 Belgian refugees of the war. Accommodation was found in five houses in West Graham Street, which were furnished by the committee.
1917	Miss Agnes C. Patterson was appointed Church Sister. (Her "visiting card" is one of the items displayed in the National Trust's tenement flat at 145 Buccleuch Street).
1918	It is recorded that 252 members were on active service in the armed forces (including 83 commissioned). 30 received awards, including a posthumous VC.
	A large Red Cross work party was active in Wellington.
	A choir of 119 performed Mendelssohn's "Elijah".
	The Primary and Junior Sunday Schools began to meet in the afternoon, while the Senior Department (over 11) met at 9.45 a.m.
1920	On Monday 26th January there was a "Welcome Home" social for ex-service personnel.
1921	A choir of 146 performed Mendelssohn's "St. Paul".
	"The Round Table" was started for Sunday evening discussions, formed from the previous Literary and Social Club, and largely led by Dr. Morrison.
	The first Christmas Dinner was provided for the children in the East Park Home in Maryhill (supported by the Sunday Schools in Wellington and the Missions).
1922	A choir of 157 performed Bach's "St. Matthew Passion" and the church was packed for two nights.
1923	Dr. Morrison preached the first sermon ever broadcast by radio in Scotland.
1924	On 21st October there was a presentation to Mr. Fred Turner after forty years' service, during which he was never absent through illness.
	A choir of 183 performed Handel's "Messiah".
1926	Dr. Morrison was appointed Moderator of the General Assembly of the United Free Church. He went on a visit to missionaries in South Africa.
	It is recorded that a staff of 300-plus was engaged in running the congregational and mission activities.

1927	In October, the Girls' Auxiliary opening meeting had a visit from Mrs. James McGregor Hart (of Wellington), the first G.A. President.

1927   In October, the Girls' Auxiliary opening meeting had a visit from Mrs. James McGregor Hart (of Wellington), the first G.A. President.

On 7th December, Dr. Morrison's semi-jubilee was celebrated.

1928   On 9th September, Sir Oliver Lodge, D.Sc., F.R.S., preached on British Association Sunday. The church was crammed, with people sitting on the pulpit steps and the hall full with the overflow.

The membership reached its maximum, 1,868; the congregational Sunday School had 38 teachers and 178 children.

On 14th October, Dr. Morrison died early on Communion Sunday morning.

1929   On Wednesday 5th June, the Rev. Ernest D. Jarvis was inducted; 1,200 signed the call. The Glasgow Herald commented on the little man with the stature of Napoleon and the jaw of iron who had dared to step into Morrison's pulpit!

The new Queen Margaret Bridge was opened over the Kelvin, and the new Hillhead High School in Oakfield Avenue was built in 1929/31.

On Sunday 6th October, the Church of Scotland was reunited and there was a Service of Thanksgiving.

1930   The United Free Church prior to the Union had two organisations for women – the Women's Foreign Mission and the Women's Home Mission Committees. On Wednesday 12th March the Wellington Branch of the Church of Scotland Woman's Guild was formed, and nearly 300 joined. The first President was Mrs. W. L. McKerrow. The Branch took over the activity of the previous Women's Committees and set up Standing Committees, I, for Home Mission work, and II, for Foreign and Jewish Mission work.

The tenth East Park Home Christmas Dinner was provided. Following the Union of the Churches, the Girls' Auxiliary became the Girls' Association.

Sunday evening meetings for men were started.

1931   On 18th March a choir of 100 performed Handel's "Messiah" to a packed church.

The Primary Sunday School for under-eights began to meet at 11.30 on Sunday mornings during the services.

1932/33   A new style of Year Book was introduced with a comprehensive guide to activities.

In February 1932 the Wellington Parish was defined as bounded by the centre of University Avenue, Hillhead Street, Bute Gardens, Cecil Street, Great Western Road and Oakfield Avenue. It did not include the University.

Mrs. Rachel Cuthbert, President of Wellington Girls' Association, became National President.

On 16th March 1932 the choir recital was of Mendelssohn's "Elijah".

1933   New arrangements were introduced for the proclamation in church of Banns of Marriage for the Registration District of Hillhead.

In June, Mr. W. L. McKerrow resigned as Sunday School Superintendent after 23 years. (He died in May 1935.) With his father William McKerrow, who died in 1912, they had given unbroken service for 78 years.

1934   The 50th anniversary of the Church building, and the completion of fifty years' service by Mr. Fred Turner as organist.

At the Special Service on Sunday 7th October, the same date exactly as the 100th Anniversary Service, the praise included the Old Hundredth and "Worship the Lord in the beauty of holiness".

On Tuesday October 9th at the Jubilee Meeting the speakers were Sir D. Y. Cameron, the Very Rev. Dr. John White, Professor J. D. Mackie of the Chair of Scottish History and Literature, who reviewed the history of the Congregation, and the Rev. A. S. Kydd, Secretary of the Foreign Missions Committee of the Church of Scotland. Dr. White recalled the opening in 1884 and particularly the minister, the architecture, and the famous collection.

Mr. Turner received a jubilee presentation.

On Sunday 14th October there were 1254 at the Communion Services.

The service on 21st October was broadcast to the Empire.

1934/35   A congregational golf club was started, but the Literary and Social Club was given up.

In 1935 the Glasgow Subway was electrified.

1936   Sunday 26th February: Memorial Service for King George V. March: Mr. Fred Turner resigned and Mr. John B. Rankin was appointed organist.

1937	Three evening services were broadcast to the Empire.
	November 1st: A new society was formed for young men and women. This, despite the interruption of the war, was to pave the way for a significant development, the Young People's Society, now the Youth Fellowship.
1938	The Fabric Fund was started to ensure the maintenance of the Church buildings by providing money for exceptional repairs.
	The Church Roll was now dropping and was at 1699.
	(The year of Glasgow's fourth great Exhibition, the remarkable Empire Exhibition in Bellahouston Park, and the year when the B.B.C. acquired Queen Margaret College by the Kelvin for their Headquarters for Scotland).
1939/45	The Second World War.
1939	On Sunday 3rd September Mr. Jarvis came into the pulpit a few minutes late to tell the congregation that the Prime Minister had announced on the wireless at 11 o'clock that this country was once again at war with Germany.
	Because of the blacking out of streets and buildings in the country to deny assistance to enemy aircraft, afternoon services were instituted for a month until mid-October. After that evening services were conducted in the hall at 6 p.m. and this arrangement continued until mid-December, by which time the Church windows had been blacked out. On 28th April 1940 the traditional time of 7 p.m. was resumed.
	The Woman's Guild began afternoon meetings. There were busy work parties on bandages and dressings for the St. Andrew's Ambulance Association, comforts for the Services, and sphagnum moss for wound dressings. Canteen services were supplied.
	The mother of a refugee gave the three-dimensional gold stars which for so many years hung on the Christmas tree in the Church.
1943	Mrs. W. L. McKerrow became National President of the Woman's Guild.
	The Girls' Association closed down.
	On 10th January, Mr. Jarvis broadcast on the Home Service.
	On 25th June Dr. Jarvis received the honorary degree of D.D. from his old University of St. Andrews.
1945	Dr. Jarvis's semi-jubilee was marked, and a presentation made to Miss Agnes C. Patterson, the Church Sister.

THE POST WAR PERIOD TO 1984

This was a time of anxiety, and not only through the social and economic problems arising from the end of hostilities and the complex process of readjustment. The life and work of Wellington was affected by what was known then as the New Society with affluence and "liberation" as its driving force and proclaimed goal. It was a time when in reaction to the restraints and disciplines of the war years, the pendulum swung away and everything that savoured of the old authoritarian ways in government, in teaching, in parenthood, in the voluntary youth organisations, and of course in the Church, came under attack and challenge to justify beliefs and methods.

Town and Country Planning, and particularly the Scottish Act of 1947, gave local planning authorities new and powerful control over development, and the area enclosed by University Avenue, Byres Road, Great George Street – both ends – and Bank Street was zoned for predominantly University purposes. The explosion in the ownership and use of motor cars and the rush of post-war housing development dispersed the Congregation. The purposes and prospects for the Mission work in Anderston rapidly diminished.

University developments, coupled with uncertainty as to their further expansion plans and timing, and historical and other factors, led to the old residential area of Hillhead – the parish in fact – declining as an area of family houses into something which professional planners called a twilight zone, being neither attractive for new private development nor earmarked for comprehensive public re-development. Its population became increasingly transient with rooming houses and students' accommodation.

Wellington's buildings were showing their age, while galloping inflation threatened the financial position of Wellington and indeed all of its members.

- - - - - - - - - - - - - - -

1946 15th May. Wellington bought 29 Lilybank Gardens from the Jarvis family and so acquired the Church Manse.

There was a major and successful effort to raise £5,000 for the National Church Extension Scheme.

Encouragement came from the enthusiasm of the Young People's Society (later the Youth Fellowship) which started up again with 98 members.

In November, Miss J. Freda S. Anderson was appointed as Wellington's first Church Secretary, and gave sterling service in that capacity. In addition, she devoted herself to caring social work of exceptional quality among the congregation.

49

THE YOUNG PEOPLE'S SOCIETY AT WISTON LODGE, 1948

BACK ROW: Evered Hart, ? McKenzie, Maxwell Hart, —————, Moira Kemp, Primrose Rutherford, —————, Kathleen Bogle, Hamish Walker, George Davidson, Tom Boyd, Hamish Service, Willie Brown.
3rd ROW: John Jarvis, Barbara ? , George ? , Margaret Maxwell, Mary Rodger, Margaret Bosomworth, Lois MacCallum, —————, Janette Copeland, Helen Henderson, Nancy Scott, Wilma McColl, Noel Henderson, Freda Anderson, Sheena Henderson, —————, Margaret ? —————, Mary Murdoch, Betty Nixon, Sandy Davidson.
2nd ROW: Stuart Henderson, Mary Cumming, Betty Humphreys, May Macfarlane, Warden of Wiston, May Peterkin, Hector McKerrow, Mrs. E. D. Jarvis, Dr. E. D. Jarvis, Jean Stark Brown, Kit Strang, Margaret Macpherson, Ian Rodger, Alison Boyd.
FRONT ROW: Margaret Cumming, Margaret Ann Hart, Jenny Macpherson, Pat Davidson, Isabel Brown, Sheena McAslan, Mayleen Henderson, Mary Pryde, May Brown.

50

1947	March-April. Three Missionary Evenings presented exhibitions and plays.
1948	The Young People's Society had a very successful residential week-end conference (the first of three) at Wiston Lodge, the YMCA camping and conference centre lying at the south foot of Tinto Hill in Lanarkshire.
1950	On 7th November the Missionary Society further amended its constitution.
	Social hours were held for young people in the vicinity.
	Dr. Jarvis was appointed Warrack Lecturer on Preaching.
	On 15th October the Northern Division of the Girl Guides Association Cadet Company to train future leaders began to meet in the Library.
1951	Anxiety about the effect of the City of Glasgow Development Plan led to the lodging of representations with the Secretary of State for Scotland.
	It is recorded that increasing numbers of children were leaving the morning service at the appropriate time to go to the Sunday School, and noticeably that families were tending to come to Church in family units, which affected activities for younger people.
	The Men's Association was revived and continued until 1962.
	The Missionary Society helped the Church Extension charge at Colston-Milton. The Whiteinch Orphanage, later Westlands Home for Girls, was "adopted" and a scheme for regular visits started.
1951/52	Mrs. Jarvis became the National President of the Woman's Guild.
	A car was bought for the minister's use – a black Wolseley saloon.
	In June, Dr. Jarvis received the honorary degree of D.D. from the University of Glasgow.
	Three elders were actively assisting the new congregation forming at Colston-Milton. Help was also given with the rapidly growing Sunday School there under the leadership of Miss Marjorie Bosomworth.
	Car parking was beginning to present difficulties in the vicinity of Wellington.
	On 31st December 1952 the Wellington Watch-Night Service was the first such service to be broadcast on television from a Glasgow church.
1952	Miss Christina Buchan's legacy was announced.

1953	On 3rd April there was a broadcast of an organ recital by Mr. Coulthard, organist of Wellington.

On 8th November the Remembrance Sunday service was broadcast for the Imperial Graves Commission. The address by Dr. Jarvis was particularly well received (in both senses) at home and overseas.

1954

It was announced that Dr. Jarvis had been nominated to be Moderator of the General Assembly, 1954.

On January 3rd at 5.25, there was a children's broadcast on the U.K. network. Pupils from Hillhead High School, Glasgow Academy and Laurel Bank School took part.

On May 11th, a congregational gathering was held to mark Dr. Jarvis's semi-jubilee and make the presentation of moderatorial robes. The speakers included Professor J. D. Mackie, University of Glasgow, Professor W. R. Forrester, University of St. Andrews, and the Rev. E. T. Vernon, Bridge of Weir, who had been a student with Dr. Jarvis at New College. The Sunday School, Hillhead High School, and the Northern Division of the Girl Guides Association made contributions to the robes.

Wellington resolved to contribute £10,000 to Church Extension in five years (being half the cost of a new Hall Church in Drumchapel), to be financed by spending some of the Missionary Society's funds, by the encouragement of donations by Deeds of Covenant, and by a general increase in congregational giving.

On May 18th, Dr. Jarvis was installed as Moderator and officially encountered Mrs. Jarvis in her third year as National President of the Woman's Guild. The congregation was kept in touch with the Moderator's programme through special leaflets, and the Very Rev. George Johnstone Jeffrey, D.D., kept Wellington's services going during the moderatorial year.

On September 12th, Dr. Jarvis gave the address at a huge Boys' Brigade Conventicle at Hampden Park to mark the centenary of the birth of Sir William A. Smith, their founder.

The Chaplain to Overseas Students, the Rev. A. Scott Hutchison, was now using Room 2 in Wellington as an office and University societies, including the Student Christian Movement, were using the hall accommodation for their meetings.

1955

On March 23rd, there was a Woman's Guild service and meeting to mark the semi-jubilee of the Wellington Branch.

March-April. The All-Scotland Crusade, with Dr. Billy

THE REV. ERNEST D. JARVIS, M.A., D.D.
Minister of Wellington 1929-58
Moderator of the General Assembly of the Church of Scotland 1954

Graham the American evangelist, was conducted at the Kelvin Hall. From May to September there were follow-up meetings and Wellington assisted with workers and accommodation.

The Colston-Milton congregation achieved full status.

The missionary effort was now linked with the Church Extension charge of Drumry St. Mary's, Drumchapel. On December 3rd the foundation stone was laid. Wellington assisted with visitation in the area of the new church.

Mrs. Jessie Dingwall succeeded Mrs. Jarvis as National President of the Woman's Guild.

On November 29th, after a plebiscite, the Annual Meeting of the Congregation approved of introducing the Weekly Freewill Offering system in the financial year 1956/57. The starting date

THE REV. STUART W. McWILLIAM, M.A., S.T.M.
Minister of Wellington 1959-72

1955   was 1st January 1957. (It had been suggested in 1942/43 to start after the war!) This led to the disappearance of the team of Lady Collectors, led by Miss Annie F. Silver, who had provided a sustained service over many years.

1956   On January 18th there was another broadcast organ recital by Mr. Coulthard.

In October there was an inconclusive plebiscite on installing a sound reinforcement system in the church.

In October Wellington was host to a meeting of the British Council of Churches, for which the improved facilities, and particularly the spacious accommodation of the new Allan Hall and Stewart Rooms, were most suitable. The Council meetings were attended by the Archbishop of Canterbury, the Right Rev. Geoffrey Fisher.

1957	The Report on the Relations between the Anglican and Presbyterian Churches, the "Bishops Report", caused a stir and much discussion.
1958	On 12th January, a certain Rev. Stuart W. McWilliam from Aberdeen was a visiting preacher.

1958 On 12th January, a certain Rev. Stuart W. McWilliam from Aberdeen was a visiting preacher.

On 3rd May, Dr. Jarvis resigned on medical advice.

The Very Rev. Dr. George Johnstone Jeffrey was appointed Interim Moderator of the Kirk Session in the vacancy.

On 27th May, at a farewell meeting, presentations were made to Dr. and Mrs. Jarvis. In tributes, the Kirk Session remarked on the way in which the Jarvis family had guided and led Wellington as pre-eminently a place of family worship, and how Dr. Jarvis had made its pulpit a place of direct and scholarly biblical teaching. No older member will ever forget the way Dr. Jarvis read from the Bible. Mrs. Jarvis was remembered as President of the Wellington Woman's Guild for eleven years and National President for four years, and for her life in Wellington and outside – a founder member of the Glasgow Tree Lovers' Society, a J.P., and much else.

On December 28th/29th, the Rev. Stuart W. McWilliam preached as sole nominee and was duly elected.

1959 On Monday 9th March, Mr. McWilliam was inducted and was welcomed at a social evening.

The old manse at 29 Lilybank Gardens was sold and a commodious ground floor flat at 59 Lauderdale Gardens in Hyndland bought as the Wellington manse.

In this year the Gilmorehill Church congregation dispersed and their church at the foot of University Avenue became a Glasgow University examination hall. A number of members transferred to Wellington.

In September, the new Church of Scotland Co-ordinated Appeal was introduced for congregational giving, to start in 1961. As a consequence, the Missionary Committee no longer had the responsibility of allocating congregational giving to the various departments of the wider work of the Church.

Dr. Jarvis presented the pulpit Bible given to him by the Sunday School in 1929.

A tape recorder was bought with funds from Miss Edgar's legacy to record services for housebound members.

1960 On Sunday 28th February, the morning service was televised (at 9.30 a.m.).

| 1960 | A major financial appeal was launched with a special booklet, seeking to raise a substantial capital sum and to effect a significant increase in the regular giving of the congregation. It was very successful.

On 1st May, the practice was introduced of carrying the offering from the collection pillars at the doors into the church for blessing at the beginning of services.

(The last tram ran on Great Western Road.)

Arrangements were made with the Corporation of Glasgow Transport Department for Sunday morning buses to run from Broomhill and Hyndland to pass Wellington in time for the morning service.

The Year Book was now separated from the Managers' Reports and Accounts and issued earlier in the autumn.

On 25th September, there was a service to mark the 400th anniversary of the Reformation – one of four broadcast services on "The Preaching of the Word".

On 10th December, the Drawing Room Music Society presented a special performance of Mozart's opera "Don Giovanni" in the Lyric Theatre in aid of the Fabric Fund (and followed this in later years with "The Marriage of Figaro", "Il Seraglio", and "Albert Herring" by Britten). |

| 1961 | *The New English Bible – New Testament* was published.

On 31st December, the morning service was recorded and the Watch Night Service televised live. |

| 1962 | The Men's Association was closed down.

The Partner Plan for contact with missionaries overseas was launched.

By September, the crypt which had been open on Sunday and Thursday evenings at the outset had come into use five nights per week, and activities were increasing under the Convenership of Mr. James S. Whitelaw.

On 1st November, lady managers were approved for the first time. (In 1963 the Board co-opted Mrs. A. Buchan and Mrs. Helen M. Dykes.) |

| 1963 | A revitalised Missionary Committee started a new series of initiatives under Mr. Ralph A. Hillis, chairman of its Executive Committee.

A Sunday morning creche and a congregational bookstall were started, and a service of accommodation and hospitality was initiated. |

56

The Finance Co-ordinating Committee was started (it grew out of the previous Joint Committee of Session and Managers) to correlate all aspects of Wellington's financial requirements and problems.

As a result of the international Freedom from Hunger Campaign the annual series of Lenten Lunches began and quickly proved to be popular congregational social events as well as an excellent source of funds for selected projects. Donations were received on the basis of the normal cost of Sunday lunch.

On 15th October, the Over-60 Club started, providing a weekly afternoon gathering for older folk, not necessarily all members of the Congregation. Mr. and Mrs. A. B. Paterson gave an imaginative lead.

In November, at the Annual Meeting, Mrs. Georgina V. A. Hill and Mrs. Helen M. Dykes were elected as lady managers.

During the year the Cadet Company of the Girl Guides Association was discontinued.

The Missionary Society's report in 1964/65 lists activity in the Crypt, Freedom from Hunger Lenten Lunches, Foreign Mission report and support of missionary partners, the Bookstall (with a "Book of the Month" recommendation), the Creche for young children during services, Hospital Visitation, Child Welfare and a Rehabilitation Service, Christmas cards, the Scottish Mental Health Flag Day, a Clothing Collection, Adventure Playground, Feed the Minds Campaign, and the sponsorship of the stay of a young African minister. 482 helpers were involved in these activities.

1964   Dr. Jarvis died on 21st January 1964. On 28th January there was a Memorial Service at 12 noon.

In April there was a Parish Visitation.

On 24th June the Congregation approved the use of funds from the James Taylor bequest to buy a top floor flat at 127 Hyndland Road as a manse for the assistant minister.

1965   On 9th March the Presbytery added the Gilmorehill Parish to Wellington's.

1966   On Sunday 27th March Mr. McWilliam's jubilee was marked. Presentations were made, and he and Mrs. McWilliam later enjoyed a visit to the Holy Land.

On November 27th, the Congregation decided that women would now be eligible for election and ordination as elders.

1966	In September the Missionary Committee's plan for sponsoring a year's stay of a young African minister came to fruition and the congregation welcomed the arrival of Saindi Chiphangwi from the Synod of Blantyre, Malawi. He was an instant success with everyone and functioned as an Assistant Minister during his stay.
1967	At a Special Meeting, women were among the new elders nominated by the congregation. Mrs. Jessie Dingwall and Mrs. Kathleen H. Philip were elected. Miss Mary W. Swanson was appointed by the Session in 1969.

June. The Rev. Saindi Chiphangwi left Scotland.

A creche for handicapped children on Fridays to relieve their parents was started in September under Mrs. Mamie Young, and did notable work.

On October 14th/15th there was a Session Conference at Dunblane. This important event saw the start of a long self-examination by Wellington of its position and role. The Congregation's purpose in serving its members and others was weighed against the rapidly changing scene in the Church vicinity, the steady move away of many of the Congregation, the disappearance of the organised mission work in Anderston and the difficulty of making effective contact with the University. It was appreciated that a day was coming when tradition and preaching alone would not sustain the Congregation. It was recognised that the enthusiasm of the Missionary Committee's recent initiatives should be more effectively underwritten, and that the Missionary Society with its Committee and Executive Committee should go, and a Projects Committee be launched. It was also decided that the Minister should join the Finance Co-ordinating Committee.

In October the Young People's Society reviewed their policy.

On November 19th and 26th and December 3rd and 10th, the B.B.C. recorded evening services for broadcasting on the four Advent Sundays.

At the Annual Meeting in November, the Congregation decided to abolish seat rents after the financial year 1967/68.

1968	On 7th January Sunday evening Communion was introduced, nine times a year at the end of the evening service.

Mr. McWilliam was appointed Warrack Lecturer on Preaching and lectured in St. Andrews and Edinburgh.

The missionary activities in Anderston which had continued after the closing down of Stobcross House in 1949 came to an end. The disappearance of the Mission together with the introduction of the Co-ordinated Appeal by the Church of Scotland led to the decision formally to abolish the Missionary Society on 8th April. Its Executive Committee became the new Projects Committee, of which the first convener was Dr. Malcolm Shaw.

On 26th May a TV recording was made in the evening for the programme "Sunday Half Hour".

In June Mr. A. N. R. Steel was appointed as the first Stewardship Promoter.

1969   On Tuesday 18th March the old link with Anderston was remembered when a Wellington gift was presented to the striking new Church there of a corner bench and table for their entrance lounge.

In September there was a Flower Festival for two days in aid of the Girls' High School, Kalimpong, India.

In November the Kirk Session decided that instead of formal morning dress which had always been worn by men when on duty as elders at Communion services, dark lounge suits would now be acceptable.

"After Meetings" in the Crypt were run as University International Club Open Nights.

1970   Mr. McWilliam was away for five months as Turnbull Lecturer in Australia. The Rev. J. Neil Alexander, M.A., B.D., S.T.M., acted as Interim Moderator.

The New English Bible – Old Testament, was published and on 16th March a copy was sent to Saindi Chiphangwi as a present. There was a further experiment – the Ichthus Group for the 14-18 year olds. (*Ichthus* is the Greek for fish, the letters of the word in Greek being the first letters of the Greek words for "Jesus Christ, Son of God, Saviour").

A series of social evenings was arranged for new members.

1971   On 31st January, the Young People's Society conducted the entire evening service: this was welcomed by the Congregation and their services became a regular feature of later years.

Still another move was made to encourage the participation of members – Forum 71: it was to cater for everyone between the YPS and the Over-60 Club!

In 1971/72 activities in the crypt, which had diminished considerably from what proved to be a too-ambitious start, now took a more structured form with the starting of a Friday

| 1971 | teenagers' club led by Mr. James S. Whitelaw and offering an attractive range of activities. |
| 1968/73 | During these years Wellington passed through a critical period. There was increasing anxiety about the relentlessly declining membership, the fall in the Congregation's regular income, and the steadily increasing cost of maintaining the Church buildings. On the other hand there were reasonable capital funds in hand and the mood was that it might be better to move while we were at strength than remain until the whole operation of Wellington on its present site became an impossible burden. It was known that the University was planning considerable expansion, and Wellington being now in effect on the University campus and within the University zone on the city's Development Plan, the only possible purchaser of Wellington's land and buildings would be the University itself. |

Confidential approaches were made to the University, starting in 1968, and by early 1971 there were encouraging indications that they were interested. There were three specific possibilities: that our buildings might become a University concert hall for its Music Department, or an auditorium for the Drama Department and in both cases it might also function as a small hall for suitable University occasions. The third possibility grew from the proposal by the Church of Scotland to give up Trinity College and the possibility of housing the Faculty of Divinity in Wellington, with perhaps the Congregation continuing. However, this latter idea was ruled out late in 1971.

At this point came a bombshell when Mr. McWilliam announced that he had received a call from Killearn Church.

A confidential paper in the name of the Session and Managers was then sent out to members, for a Special Meeting immediately following the Annual Meeting in November, and read as follows:

> By a remarkable coincidence, the Session and Managers had decided to put urgent proposals for the future of Wellington before the congregation only a few days before our Minister's announcement of his invitation to preach as sole nominee in the vacancy at Killearn. He will be greatly missed; but his departure will have the effect of throwing stronger light on the critical position already facing us.
>
> Here it is in a nutshell:–
>
> (a) Our numbers are steadily dwindling. The University encroaches increasingly on the old residential area of Hillhead. Our numbers are falling for a variety of reasons and the new

members are not of sufficient number to fill the gap. Fewer children and young people come to Wellington. These are conditions which impose an unfair strain on the Minister, since only the sustained abilities of an outstanding preacher will hold a scattered congregation together and bring in new members.

(b)   The traditional generosity of Wellington members has kept up our giving despite our declining numbers, and our record of financial giving to the Church at large is perhaps unsurpassed in the Church of Scotland. But that is not enough. While our average giving per member during the past year has been maintained, falling membership has prevented us increasing it and so we have been unable to meet both the increased costs of running Wellington and the increased calls by the Church of Scotland. As a result our accounts for the past year show a large deficit. Without an increase in giving which must be supported by an increase in membership there can be no improvement in the future of our financial position. If the decline in members continues it could become very serious in a year or two, even although we reduced our giving to the Schemes of the Church of Scotland.

(c)   Our magnificent building dating from 1884, presents an increasing problem of upkeep; essential maintenance is looming at a cost of thousands of pounds, and major overhauls to the fabric will erode the Fabric Fund, presenting future members with the acute problem of raising substantial sums to provide for future years in respect of the building alone, quite apart from the every-day running of the congregation.

WHAT SHOULD WE DO?

There are three choices:–

(1)   Move, as our predecessors did twice before, from Anderston to Wellington Street, and thereafter to Hillhead.

(2)   Remain where we are;

  or

(3)   Close down.

The Session and Managers have met together anxiously to consider these possibilites.

(3)   This would mean selling our building, paying over our accumulated funds including the proceeds of sale to the Church of Scotland, and all of us dispersing to join other churches.

The Session and Managers, conscious of the long tradition of Wellington, feel confident that this proposal could only be acceptable to the Congregation in the last resort and consequently they have discarded it.

61

(2) Would involve a calculated risk in defying the conditions listed above which have already brought Wellington close to a crisis, and which could intensify should membership further decrease. Is it a duty and a challenge to maintain Wellington in the heart of the University? The population of the academic and student body may need our services, but will not provide a stable financial contribution on the scale required, so that the increasing burden of maintaining the work and buildings of Wellington would fall on a congregation declining both in numbers and resources and it is likely that the healthy balance of people of different resources and backgrounds, which has been one of the great strengths of Wellington, will be upset by the dispersal of the congregation over an ever wider area, and the natural inclination of children and young people to want to join a neighbourhood church. The Session and Managers realise what a wrench it would be to contemplate leaving University Avenue and disposing of our building, but on mature consideration feel that this is the time to face a move, rather than some years hence when there could be serious deterioration in all aspects of Wellington's position.

This leads to (1) – a Move.

When our forefathers faced this, Glasgow was expanding, and moreover the old U.P. Church was both confident and competitive in venturing into recently developed areas. We could only encounter something approaching this atmosphere by attempting to set up a new Wellington Church in an outlying area, such as one of the great housing estates; but that would in effect disperse our own congregation, and would be no different from choice number (3) above in serving the Church as a whole.

If we wish to seek to retain as many of our present members as possible – and that is surely a worthy goal – we would need to re-establish ourselves in an area convenient to them. Research shows that the most convenient point of assembly for our present members from their homes would be in the Hyndland area. But it would be inconceivable in these days to contemplate encroachment on the parishes or territories of other churches, or the irresponsibility of spending an enormous sum of money to build a new church when there are so many church buildings already and these in most cases so sadly underused. Moreover, there could not be sufficient funds to finance an independent development on the scale required.

Much would depend on what could be obtained for our present site and buildings, and town planning and practical factors make it self-evident that the only prospect of sale at all is to the University. It is known from approaches made that they would be prepared to consider buying Wellington for use by one or more University departments: the price they would pay would be that agreed with the Government District Valuer on the basis of current market value, and at this stage it is impossible to estimate what that might be, although we are confident it would be a considerable sum.

These factors lead to the suggestion that we might seek amalgamation with an existing congregation, or more than one congregation, in the Hillhead or Hyndland areas, on the basis that an existing church would provide the place of worship, while the financial resources we would be able to take with us would enable a major improvement or development of ancillary accommodation to be made, to the intent that we would achieve a vital church for Sundays and a modern activities centre throughout the week, located in the heart of a residential area and more convenient for access by public and private transport from most of the areas in which our present members reside. It is interesting to record that a move of this type would be in line with current thinking about the role and mission of the Church of Scotland in the years ahead.

This clearly poses practical, technical and personal problems, not the least of which is the effect of such a proposal on our authority – and ability – to call a new Minister, and there is the conflict between the urgency imposed by our situation and the need for time to enable wise steps to be taken in necessary sequence.

The Session and Managers accordingly, relying on the loyalty and generosity of the congregation, commend to the congregation the following resolutions which will be put at a Special Meeting of the congregation:–

(1) That the appropriate steps be taken without delay to seek and call a Minister whose preaching calibre and personal qualities of organisation and service would commend themselves to the congregation and who would be prepared to come on the basis that he and the congregation would work together at the outset to sustain Wellington on its present site for at least such time as proves to be necessary to enable a wise move to be arranged.

(2) That the University authorities be advised that, provided a satisfactory price and convenient date of sale were offered, the Trustees and Managers would have the authority of the congregation to negotiate for the disposal of the site and buildings to the University, the final decision to be made (as required by our Constitution) by the congregation at a Special Meeting.

(3) That immediate steps be taken, in consultation with the Presbytery of Glasgow and with the office-bearers of the congregations of other churches in our area, to explore the possibility of an amalgamation and development to create a modern Church centre in the Hyndland or Hillhead area.

"The Session and Managers are confident that these steps could lead to significant and indeed exciting results for the Church in the west end of Glasgow."

Unfortunately, despite its marking as strictly confidential, this leaflet was "leaked" to the "Glasgow Herald", resulting in an article on 29th November, and comment later in *Life and Work*.

A letter had to be sent to the Editors to correct the impression that Wellington was about to collapse!

The three resolutions were duly passed by a full meeting.

Meantime the Rev. John L. Kent, D.D., was appointed Interim Moderator in the vacancy.

On 12th January, just before Mr. McWilliam's last Sunday, there was a farewell meeting. The President of the YPS spoke of his success with young people, his inspiration and his fearlessness. A senior elder disclosed his life-long interest in preaching and ranked Mr. McWilliam high as having outstanding gifts as a preacher.

An interesting matter was resolved at this time, in that after taking the opinion of the Procurator of the Church of Scotland, the Session and Managers advised the congregation in April that the long tradition in Wellington of not having its Minister present at the congregation's Annual Meeting was unsound in law and should cease. This clearing of the air was of no little help to the Vacancy Committee in their task of finding a minister of sufficient calibre to suit Wellington and courage to come in this time of an uncertain future.

There then followed a strangely unreal period. There was no clear response from the University although the Government District Valuer proceeded to value the property to see what compensation might be offered for its acquisition and to cover the disturbance of a move.

The effect of all this on the Congregation was electrifying. There was a remarkable display of corporate morale.

In 1972/73 lunches were provided on Thursdays for University students, initially under the intriguing title of "Bread and Circus". This was to lead to a major activity later.

In August Dr. S. Forbes Pearson, an elder, with a team of helpers launched Park Week, a missionary effort, as someone said, "to run a seaside mission in Kelvingrove Park." This, in which other churches round about helped, started a completely

THE REV. MAXWELL D. CRAIG, M.A., B.D., Th.M.
Minister of Wellington 1973–

new tradition in missionary outreach and a regular series of summer events which, with the other activities which grew out of it, at last showed signs of providing the area of service which had eluded Wellington since the Anderston mission work ended. Still more vitally, a growing band of younger people began taking an active role in the Congregation. The Pearson family made a major and sustained contribution to these developments.

1973   The Rev. Maxwell D. Craig from Grahamston, Falkirk, was put forward as sole nominee and preached on 22nd October 1972: he was welcomed, and inducted on 17th January 1973. Dense fog sadly prevented a party coming from Falkirk to wish their former minister well in his new charge. On Monday 18th January there was a very happy social to enable Mr. Craig to meet the Congregation. Among other items there was a display in the hall of records and pictures telling the story of Wellington in outline.

Discussions of a somewhat tentative nature opened at a meeting on 30th March 1973, under the aegis of the Presbytery, with the other churches in the west end, to discover whether there was an over-all plan to rationalise the organisation of the many churches in the area, into which one of the Wellington options might have fitted. Sadly, these discussions were non-productive, but close contacts were opened between Wellington, Belmont-Hillhead, and Kelvinside Churches, all of whom had similar problems, and this led to further discussions.

On 14th March 1973 all the Church organisations combined to present a Mission and Service evening in Wellington.

At Easter Mr. Craig introduced and led a further new tradition – an Easter Day Service early in the morning at the top of Dumgoyne above the Blane Valley – an occasion welcomed by the increasing number of young folk, and by not a few old-timers, and a source of real inspiration.

In May, Mr. Craig went to Belfast for a spell to relieve a Belfast minister for a holiday. The Irish troubles were at their height and the Congregation's prayers went with him for a safe return.

In June, *The Church Hymnary, Third Edition* was published and adopted for use in Wellington. The Congregation missed some of their favourite psalms and hymns, but faithfully learned and enjoyed some of the new material.

July saw the visit of 17 boys and girls from Belfast for a week's holiday with Wellington families: they had a splendid time.

In September, the Session met in conference at Churches' House, Dunblane, and considered current opportunities to respond to the challenge of the University setting, the best type of mission for us, and the possibility of starting up youth organisations.

In September, too, the manse at 59 Lauderdale Gardens was sold and a new manse at 27 Kingsborough Gardens purchased.

On October 29th an important report, "Statistical and Financial Information, 1956-1972" was presented to the Session and Managers by Mr. Kenneth W. Fyfe and Mr. John Duncan. This analysed the Congregation's structure and resources, and after revealing that the membership had been steady at around 1,500 from 1956 to 1964, but was now declining at 4% per annum, pointed out that if the decline continued at the same rate it would mean our membership reaching zero by 1988. Despite generous and increased giving by members, the financial position was relentlessly deteriorating so that capital funds would be eroded and the interest on them lost. As a result our giving to the wider work of the Church would have to be cut back. The Report stressed that an increase in membership was the only long-term solution.

At this juncture the Session, under Mr. Craig's leadership, decided to make a Statement of Policy as follows:

> Approved by the Kirk Session at its meeting on 6th November 1973, and to be made by the minister at the Annual General Meeting on 27th November.
>
> 1. The members of Wellington are in a state of uncertainty. And with reason. At the Annual General Meeting of 1971 three resolutions were passed:–
>
> > (a) to call a minister on the basis that he and the congregation would work together at the outset to sustain Wellington on its present site for at least such time as proves to be necessary to enable a wise move to be arranged.
> >
> > (b) that the University authorities be advised that provided a price and date could be agreed, the Managers would have authority to negotiate for the sale of the site and buildings to the University, the final decision to be made by the Congregation at a special meeting.
> >
> > (c) that immediate steps be taken, in consultation with the Presbytery and with other congregations in the area to explore the possibility of an amalgamation or any other development to create a modern Church Centre in the Hyndland or Hillhead area.
>
> All three of these resolutions have been carried out. A minister has been called. The University authorities have been approached; the District Valuer has visited

Wellington; and nothing more has been heard. The inference is that the University do not, in the foreseeable future, intend to respond to our approach. Accordingly, the modern Church Centre, without the sum anticipated from the University, ceases to be an option. But the atmosphere of uncertainty remains in the congregation and requires to be dispelled.

At precisely this juncture a Statistical and Financial Report on Wellington, prepared by two Managers, Ken Fyfe and John Duncan, was made to a meeting of 56 Elders and Managers on 29th October. It is a report which cannot be ignored.

2.   We intend to resume the initiative, and to take action to maintain and to develop the life and witness of Wellington on its present site.

3.   The Kirk Session has identified three objectives which follow from the intention expressed in paragraph 2:–

(a) Externally, we are on a strategic site, both in relation to the life of the University at our doorstep and in relation to the area of the Park Ward, with its particular needs. We shall develop the potential of our site in both these directions.

(b) Internally, we shall review our life and work within the congregation – i.e. we shall review what is done each Sunday and weekday on our premises – in order to equip us for the effective execution of our role as a congregation of Christian men and women.

(c) This role will involve continuing discussion and further joint ventures with our neighbouring Churches. We welcome this involvement and look forward to our continuing co-operation with them and to its development.

4.   In order to implement these objectives, the Kirk Session has decided to establish an Objectives Committee on the lines of the committee or "cabinet" envisaged at the joint meeting of Elders and Managers held on 29th October. This Committee will consist of three Elders who will serve for a term of three years subject to annual review; two Managers serving on the same basis; and the Minister, ex officio. The Committee will have powers to co-opt, to consult and to delegate.

5. It is essential that all members of the congregation shall be kept informed both about the overall policy of the congregation as it develops, and about the week-to-week execution of that policy. Particular attention will be paid to communication, in order that the whole congregation may feel they have a part in our renewed purpose.

This was duly welcomed at the Annual Meeting: and the floodlighting was on!

By the end of 1973 there was still no sign of interest from the University, and it was known that they had new problems of finance and development to face. Likewise it was increasingly evident that of the neighbourhood churches, Belmont-Hillhead and Kelvinside were drawing together. Their ultimate union as Kelvinside-Hillhead Parish Church was announced on 18th May 1978.

1974   In March there was a Parish Visitation.

In addition to the Easter morning climb on Dumgoyne, a party of young people went to Iona – the first of frequent visits by congregational groups.

Now came another major event. It was almost as though Wellington, remaining independently on the University hill, and the possible opportunity of amalgamating with congregations to the west being at least for the foreseeable future remote, was to turn east towards the Park area for its new ally in the cause of continuing witness.

Early in this year, the office-bearers of Woodlands Church opened negotiations with Wellington. It emerged that they were facing up to the same situation as had alarmed Wellington, only their crisis point had come sooner. Discussions proceeded in the happiest way, and by April a draft Basis of Union was produced, which on Sunday 5th May was approved at Special Meetings of both Congregations and then approved by the Presbytery on 14th May. On Thursday 30th May there was a Service of Union in Wellington Church, conducted by the Presbytery. On 2nd and 9th June Communion Services were held, first in Woodlands and then in Wellington. This important development is mentioned again in the chapter about Woodlands Church. The Congregation welcomed the Rev. John A. Grimson as Associate Minister.

The membership at 30th September 1974 rose from 939 to 1,159.

THE REV. JOHN A. GRIMSON, M.A.
Associate Minister 1974–

1974 In September a Special Meeting of the united congregation approved of the sale of Woodlands Church to the congregation of St. Jude's Free Presbyterian Church, who were to move out from their building at 278 West George Street, at a price of £35,000. In accordance with their tradition they did not want either the organ or the fine stained glass windows.

The triangular-shaped piece of ground behind the church and opening off Woodlands Gate was retained for possible future sale, and leased to the purchasers in the meantime at a nominal rent.

On 8th November, Wellington was host to a Presentation Ceremony to mark the retirement of Dr. William Barclay as Professor of New Testament Language and Literature at Glasgow University. His reputation as a Bible teacher and popular communicator of the Christian gospel through books, radio and television had become legendary.

In November the Congregation bought a Ford Transit 17-seat minibus which over several years offered numerous services – transporting people from the Woodlands area to church, assisting the youth organisations, taking parties to Iona, and many more.

1974/75   The youth organisations from Woodlands – the 6th Glasgow Group, The Scout Association (Cub Scouts and later Scouts) and the 210th Glasgow Company, the Girl Guides Association, were re-established in the Woodlands Hall, while the 6th (Woodlands) Company, the Girls' Brigade, continued at Oakbank School until 1983.

In 1974/75 when Professor John Aitchison was the Projects Committee Convener, there was a further extension of work among the young people of the parish. A youth club was started for juniors on Tuesdays, and the Friday club continued for seniors. This programme called for devoted and patient service which was sustained despite anxiety and setbacks.

Arising from the friendly conversations between the three Hillhead Churches, these congregations met together for services in their different buildings in turn. In September 1974 there was a Harvest Thanksgiving Service in Belmont-Hillhead; on 27th April 1975 Wellington was at home to the others. As Glasgow was celebrating its 800 years as a Royal Burgh, the service which was attended by the Lord Provost, adopted as its theme "Glasgow 800". There was a special order of service and a remarkable exhibition in the Church of memorabilia relating to the growth of the City, and Hillhead and the University in particular. The third service on 14th September 1975 was in Kelvinside Church.

1975   The first of a series of parish visitations including the former Woodlands parish area, well organised by Professor John Aitchison, was launched as OPUS 75 – "Our Parish and Us". There was a briefing meeting on Wednesday 11th June and the visits, in which many of the congregation participated, started in September.

At this time Wellington folk, under the lead from their Minister, became increasingly committed to the work of the International Flat at 20 Glasgow Street near the Church, run by the remarkable Miss Stella Reekie, missionary and deaconess of the Church of Scotland, who had been commissioned to work among Asian families in Glasgow. Her language schools, children's play schemes, and pioneering work with the Sharing of Faiths movement earned her the love of new communities in the city.

1975	The practice was started of having "Events of the Week" leaflets for issue to members every Sunday. This was one of the factors that had a significant effect on what was already beginning to be seen as a revival of confidence in the congregation, with much more interest and participation by members than had been the case for many years. The growing sense of fellowship was aided by the starting of "coffee in the crypt" after the morning service on 20th April. This was appreciated by more and more members so that the Hall had to be used and is now filled with a happy gathering every Sunday. On 2nd June 1975 Mr. Grimson's semi-jubilee in the ministry was marked by a delightful party in the Woodlands Hall. "This is Your Life", the television programme, was skilfully adapted to bring to Wellington friends from several connections associated with Mr. Grimson as family man and as school and hospital chaplain, to confront him with their memories. Mr. and Mrs. Grimson went off for a visit to Greece and the Holy Land with the Congregation's best wishes.

In the summer of 1975 Wellington found itself considerably affected by the Hillhead Traffic Management Plan, with its one-way maze and in particular the restriction of entry into the Hillhead area from Great Western Road to Byres Road in the west and Otago Street in the east, and "residents' bays" in some of the streets. Members adapted quickly but while there were no serious problems on Sundays, there was increasing difficulty for weekday functions including weddings and special services.

October: When the Thursday lunches for students began again, they were called "Table Talk".

On 11th November the centenary of the opening of Woodlands Church would have been celebrated, and this was duly recorded in the Church Notes.

1975/76	These dates are on the cover of the last Year Book in the old style, which had become too expensive. It was decided to issue a Report from the Session and the Managers with the annual accounts for the congregation's financial year, and to have a separate Directory of activities, office-bearers, teachers and committees.

1976	On 18th January the Young People's Society conducted their annual service.

On 29th January Mr. John L. Adamson died (an elder since 1937). For many years he had made the arrangements for elders' duties at Communion services. He left a generous legacy to be used by the Projects Committee for Wellington purposes.

1976	On 5th and 6th March the Kirk Session had another weekend conference at Churches House, Dunblane.

OPUS 76 followed up the parish visitation begun last year.

In June the Young People's Society changed its name to the Youth Fellowship and came in line with the name used throughout the Church of Scotland.

During the summer Mr. Craig and his family were on a visit to the U.S.A.

In September, "Forum" having been dropped, "The Open Circle" was started to provide a centre of interest with a similar aim and invited age-range.

On 2nd October, the 210th Company of the Girl Guides held a buffet dinner in Wellington to celebrate their 50th anniversary.

1977 In January, the 6th Glasgow Scouts re-started.

To mark the Week of Prayer for Christian Unity two interesting visitors occupied the pulpit on the evenings of 16th January and 23rd January respectively; the Right Rev. Professor Thomas F. Torrance, Moderator of the General Assembly and distinguished theologian, and the Very Rev. Archbishop Thomas Winning, Roman Catholic Archbishop of Glasgow.

March 5th/6th brought another Session conference at Dunblane.

OPUS 77 completed the follow-up to the OPUS 75 and OPUS 76 parish investigations.

In September an appeal went out for increased giving and the Congregation responded generously.

On 18th November the 2nd Company, The Girls' Brigade, celebrated their 75th anniversary.

Wellington's increasing involvement in community work locally was enlarged by the appointment of representatives to the Hillhead Community Council and to the Hillhead Housing Association Ltd., incorporated to provide housing for the elderly.

1978 On 1st January the ancient system of Proclamation of Banns was discontinued.

In February and March the Glasgow Society of Organists presented four promenade organ recitals in Wellington.

There was a noticeable rise in the range of activities and service of young people in the Congregation.

In October the major decision was made to provide Students' Lunches daily in the Crypt. This required a new level of help

1978	and many members rallied to assist Mrs. Ann Wilson, an elder since 1977, who convened the enterprise. The good lunches and the friendly atmosphere attracted a steady and appreciative company of regular patrons, and provided by far the most effective and sustained contact yet with the University student community.
	In October the Cub Scouts of the 6th Glasgow distinguished themselves by winning the Cub Scout "Cooks of the Year" competition in London, and appeared in the national "Scouting" magazine.
	On Remembrance Sunday new colours were presented in Church to the Scouts and Cub Scouts.
	After twelve years service, the Friday Creche for handicapped children was given up.
1979	There was an interesting experiment with June services at 10 a.m., but this was not repeated.
	In September there was a family visit to Iona, with 48 taking part.
1980	Elders' district meetings were held in homes throughout the congregational area and were happy occasions.
	The minibus had become expensive to operate and was sold. In six years it had done 53,000 miles.
	In March there was another visit by distinguished preachers. On 9th March Archbishop Winning returned to give the address, while on 16th March the Right Rev. Robin S. Barbour, the Moderator, preached. These services attracted many visitors, as did those in 1977.
	On 12th March the Wellington Branch of the Woman's Guild marked its Golden Jubilee and provided cushions for the three chairs at the Communion Table.
	A Wellington party had a holiday in Austria and West Germany and in particular visited the Oberammergau Passion Play.
	During the summer there was a major innovation in the launching of the Alongsiders project. Two young people from Wellington were invited to spend the summer in Christian fellowship with the First Presbyterian Church in Fresno, California, and to join in the activities of the congregation there.
	On October 26th, the Right Rev. Lord Coggan, P.C., D.D. (formerly the Archbishop of Canterbury) visited an exhibition in Wellington of Christian literature in connection with the "Feed the Minds Campaign", and gave the address at the evening service.

| 1981 | The opportunity came to sell the Woodlands Gate site for a development of new flats and a price of £20,000 was obtained. On 26th April the Youth Fellowship's service was conducted in the morning. |

1981   The opportunity came to sell the Woodlands Gate site for a development of new flats and a price of £20,000 was obtained. On 26th April the Youth Fellowship's service was conducted in the morning.

In June a new bus service was arranged to run to Wellington from Knightswood via Jordanhill, Broomhill and Hyndland on Sunday mornings.

In the summer of 1981 the pace of youth work and participation quickened. It was decided to abandon the long-established practice of having a lull during what was in effect the school holiday period of July and August, and to provide events and activities throughout the summer.

The Alongsider project now came to Wellington on the initiative of the Projects Committee and was co-ordinated by Stephen Pearson and staffed by Katherine McMillan and Stephen Clarke, and bringing Diane Williams and Brian Fowler from Fresno, California. The team stayed with members of the Congregation, and there were visits to housebound members, workshops, music, drama, gardening, housegroups, Bible study, and children's activities.

There was a Congregational Conference at Dunblane on 18th-20th September.

It was observed that the Sunday School numbers were now steadily declining.

1982   On 24th January B.B.C. TV came to Wellington for two special services. In the morning there was a live broadcast of an interdenominational service for the Scout Association (marking its 75th anniversary), attended by the new Chief Scout, Major General Michael Walsh. David Kossoff gave the address. In the evening a "Songs of Praise" service was recorded for transmission on Sunday 18th April. Other local churches, five schools, the Roman Catholic chaplaincy, the University Chapel Choir and Queen's College all participated in the broadcast.

On 30th January a concert in the hall raised funds for the Prince and Princess of Wales Hospice, Glasgow's wedding present to the Prince and Princess. Wellington raised £1,614 out of a Glasgow Presbytery total of £12,500.

"Wavelength" started on Sunday 9th May – a new group for service and for learning more about Christianity.

The 2nd Glasgow Girls' Brigade (ex 8th Company Girls' Guildry) celebrated their 80th birthday. Miss Hose had been the Company Captain for 35 years.

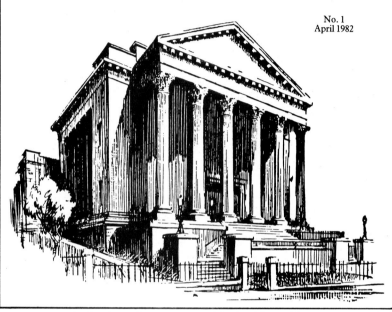

WELLINGTON
ONE HUNDRED

(Bulletin of the Centenary Celebrations Committee)

No. 1
April 1982

1982   The Summer Programme with the Alongsiders was expanded. There was another visit to Iona in April for a teenage group.

In September there was a unique Memorial Service for Stella Reekie, who had died at the peak of her work for the international community. Wellington was packed, and a moving tribute was paid by Mr. Balwant Singh Saggu, a leading member of the Sikh community.

The Hillhead Housing Association after much preparatory work acquired the block of 132 University Place and 96-140 Byres Road to develop, with first-floor flats for the elderly. This enterprise had been formed by representatives of Wellington,

Hillhead Baptist Church, The University of Glasgow and the Hillhead Community Council.

As the centenary approached, there was the first issue of a series of "Wellington One Hundred" notes in April 1982.

1983   On 6th February the morning service was conducted throughout by four Elders, and was well received by the Congregation.

Sadly, the Scout Troop had to be abandoned temporarily in March because of dwindling numbers.

The Alongsiders were with us again, with Wilma Smith as a co-ordinator. There was a large congregation on Fair Sunday in July (a new experience!) and ceilidhs, art appreciation, outings for older people, and extended visiting of members were added to the previous year's programme.

In October a successful Centenary Jumble Sale was run to "prime the pump" for the Centenary Fete planned for next June.

On November 20th the Glasgow Tree Lovers' Society celebrated their Golden Jubilee at the evening service. The Society began when some trees were cut down in University Avenue, and Mrs. E. D. Jarvis was one of the founder members.

A week later, on 27th November, a family lunch was offered in the Crypt, and no less than 180 people came along.

At the end of the year the Youth Fellowship restated their aims:

> to encourage all members to Bible study and prayer on their own and in groups;
>
> to encourage each member to full and active membership of the Church;
>
> to become involved in missionary work at home and overseas;
>
> to encourage fellowship and concern for others in their group,
>
> and to encourage evangelism both at personal level and as a group.

As well as the regular Sunday meetings there were six groups working in visiting the elderly, working with mentally handicapped, taking part in morning services at Gartnavel Hospital, helping round the church buildings, book reviews, and working with alcoholics at Kirkhaven and Westercraigs.

1984   The centenary events are recorded on pages 101–107.

The Youth Fellowship service was on 20th February.

WELLINGTON CHURCH, GLASGOW
CENSUS OF CHURCH ATTENDANCE – March 1984

	1. MORNING					2. Total Evening Attendance (Incl. those attending both services)					3. EVENING ONLY					TOTAL 1+3	AV. 1+3
	SUNDAYS 4	11	18	25	TOTAL	SUNDAYS 4	11	18	25	TOTAL	SUNDAYS 4	11	18	25	TOTAL		
MALE																	
Under 15	22	22	23	8	75	–	2	–	1	3	–	2	–	–	2	77	19
15–19	13	8	5	6	32	4	2	3	2	11	2	–	1	1	4	36	9
20–29	27	29	15	17	88	15	13	14	20	62	10	2	9	11	32	120	30
30–44	22	20	13	6	61	7	10	4	7	28	2	5	3	3	13	74	19
45–64	46	45	23	25	139	15	7	10	10	42	5	1	2	3	11	150	37
Over 65	36	42	23	26	127	9	1	2	6	18	4	–	–	2	6	133	33
Total Males	166	166	102	88	522	50	35	33	46	164	23	10	15	20	68	590	147
FEMALE																	
Under 15	31	22	23	18	94	1	–	–	–	1	1	–	–	–	1	95	24
15–19	19	11	6	7	43	7	2	2	2	13	4	–	–	–	4	47	12
20–29	49	38	26	21	134	29	21	16	24	90	12	8	10	9	39	173	43
30–44	42	31	23	12	108	6	7	3	2	18	2	5	2	2	11	119	30
45–64	84	86	48	43	261	20	16	12	15	63	5	8	6	8	27	288	72
Over 65	114	150	100	85	449	14	10	11	7	42	6	3	6	–	15	464	116
Total Females	339	338	226	186	1089	77	56	44	50	227	30	24	24	19	97	1186	297
OVERALL TOTAL	505*	504†	328	274	1611	127	91	77	96	391	53	34	39	39	165	1776	444

* Special Centenary Baptismal Service – actual attendance probably over 600.

† Communion Services morning and afternoon.

1984   During March there was a revealing census of church attendance taken for the National Bible Society of Scotland and the analysis of the results in Wellington is shown opposite.

A new and effective service was developed, co-ordinated by Edward Harvie (Elder 1964), namely, the Woodlands/Hillhead Unemployment Project. At a time when unemployment was having a demoralising effect on families and communities, the objectives were to provide actual employment, and to ascertain the needs of those living in our community and bring help. From 11th April, 1983 to 24th February, 1984 a full-time supervisor and five part-time staff were engaged to conduct a household survey in the Woodlands/Hillhead and also in the Garnethill areas. 26 households asked for help for such matters as painting rooms and reducing draughts, and the Manpower Services Commission was approached for tradesmen and helpers for this. Window-cleaners were also sought. Talks were given on the prevention of hypothermia. A useful teach-in for the 10% unemployed persons in our area was organised. This work continued.

The Lenten lunches were again well supported and £722 was raised: it was agreed to add this sum to the funds raised by the Centenary events as described later.

On 27th May the former Moderator of the General Assembly, the Very Rev. Dr. J. Fraser McLuskey, M.C., D.D., preached at the morning service. (He is the minister of St. Columba's, Pont Street, London, whose own Church's centenary service on 21st March 1984 was attended by Her Majesty the Queen).

Owing to a scare about asbestos in the roofs, the Bute and Randolph Halls of the University had to be closed on short notice, and Wellington, which had on several occasions over the years enjoyed the hospitality of the University during overhaul of the Church interior, found itself able in turn during June and July to accommodate Graduation Ceremonies on six days, including the ceremony for honorary degrees on 20th June. The Journal of the Graduates' Association recorded that numbers had unfortunately to be limited but "the splendidly coloured Commemoration Day procession descending the steps from the classical facade offered much consolation."

The Summer Programme was livelier than ever and ran from mid-June. There were further visitors from overseas including Andreas Kågedal from Sweden and a party of eight from Palmer, Alaska, U.S.A., led by their pastor, who helped to extend the programme in August.

1984   There were further congregational lunches in the crypt on 17th June, 15th July and 12th August, and these attracted full attendances and provided a further potent link in the growing sense of fellowship in Wellington. The August lunch was attended by some of a group of Americans from Presbyterian Churches who were journeying round Western and Eastern Europe, Kenya, Egypt and the Holy Land, meeting Church leaders in many parts of Christ's world-wide Church.

It was decided that starting on the first Sunday of September, the Congregation would sing the Psalms from the Psalter instead of the selection of fifty placed within the body of the Hymn Book "CH3".

The Congregation entered upon its hundredth year of worship and service in its present building, very conscious of its traditions, but resolved to look forward and with the help of the Holy Spirit to create something new, distinctive and relevant in the years to come.

MISSION HALLS, PICCADILLY STREET

Home Mission Work in Anderston

Anderston was where the Congregation began, and from the earliest years the active work of mission there was the hallmark of the Church's work.

When the first move was made over the short distance to Wellington Street in 1827, the work in Anderston was uninterrupted, and on 23rd November 1835 the congregation constituted itself as a Missionary Society to involve the whole of the membership in the support of the wider work of the Church at home and overseas. The building-up of activity including the starting of Sunday Schools and Day Schools has already been mentioned.

In 1854 the Mission Hall at 21/25 Piccadilly Street was erected, only a few yards from the site of the original church in Cheapside Street: the title was taken in name of John Scott and others as Trustees for the Congregation in 1856, and later transferred to the Trustees for Wellington Church under the 1885 constitution. The building was opened on 7th June 1858, and for a time was the hub of the missionary work in the area.

In 1874 a brick church was erected in Lancefield Street further west on a site held by Trustees for the Missionary Committee, to accommodate the increasing work in the Cranstonhill district, and a new congregation – the "Cranstonhill U.P." – was formed with Wellington's support. In 1885 this congregation asked liberty to build a new place of worship on Wellington's site at Lancefield Street and agreed to pay off the existing loan. After anxious discussion about fund-raising, procedure, and control of development, the Wellington Congregation approved of a gift of the property to Trustees for the Cranstonhill congregation.

In 1887 improvements were authorised by the congregation to the Piccadilly mission buildings.

Then came a momentous development. In 1889, Mr. Alexander Allan chaired a committee on the accommodation needs for mission work in Anderston. This led to the purchase of ground in Cranstonhill from the Town Council through the Police Commissioners at the corner of 185 Stobcross Street and 51 Lancefield Street, and the erection of a large suite of mission halls and rooms. This building was provided and fully equipped by Mr. Allan and gifted to the Congregation of Wellington, who took possession on 5th September 1890. The new halls were named "Stobcross House".

A year later Mr. Allan's son, Robert S. Allan, bought and made available for several years another hall adjoining the Piccadilly mission.

Thus were established the bases for the two mission centres known for many years to Wellington folk as "Piccadilly" and "Cranstonhill", and the Missionary Society was substantially geared to the organisation and control of the two mission centres.

There was a moment of anxiety about the structure of Stobcross House in 1891 when the Caledonian Railway was digging the tunnels for the low level line from Glasgow Central under Anderston to Partick and Dumbarton.

In 1907 we read that the "Sabbath School Society" appointed by the congregation controlled both the Congregational Sabbath Schools at Wellington and the work at the Missions: the report of that year calls for more leaders. This organisation disappeared in 1931 when the re-organisation took place, after which control was direct by independent committees for the two missions.

In 1929 the district began to change with a big slum clearance scheme in Anderston.

In 1931, at the request of the Presbytery, there was a linking-up of the work of the Cranstonhill Mission with St. Mark's-Lancefield Church: a new committee was set up with members from the recently united St. Mark's-Lancefield congregation and from Trinity College Glasgow Students' Missionary Society.

This in turn led to 1936, when the Piccadilly congregation was separated, and the Piccadilly and Cranstonhill Missions were amalgamated in Stobcross House, which was now called "Wellington Halls".

In 1937, after substantial reconstruction and redecoration, Wellington Halls were re-opened and dedicated on Sunday 7th February as the sole centre for Wellington's Home Mission work.

The old halls at Piccadilly Street were sold, together with a tenement at Clydeferry Street, to the Queen Margaret Settlement Association.

In 1949, in the conditions prevailing in the city centre after the war, the steady decline in the operation of the Anderston mission came to a head. The Home Board of the Church of Scotland was unwilling to take over responsibility, and indeed the running of separate missions by congregations was seen to be increasingly inappropriate and in rapidly changing social conditions even unacceptable. There was anxious discussion about the right course of action, and eventually, fortified by a learned opinion of no less than four Sheriffs who were members of the

MISSION HALLS, CRANSTONHILL

congregation at the time that it was in order to do so, the buildings were sold to the Boys' Brigade for use by them as a training centre. They were later acquired by the Corporation of Glasgow and after a short period when they were leased to Scottish Opera as rehearsal rooms and stores, the buildings were demolished in the course of the building of the Kingston Bridge and its approach roads.

It is impossible to gauge and still more impossible to appraise the total effort that went into the Home Mission work in Anderston, lovingly sustained over so many years in the interests not of collective achievement capable of recording but of caring work with countless individuals whose lives, together with those of the Wellington folk who served there, were enriched by that experience. There can be no doubt that the sustained service of a remarkable number of loyal and faithful Wellington members brought the message of the Gospel, and opened windows of fellowship and widened horizons for shuttered lives, for un-numbered children, young people and grown-ups.

Incidentally, the unusual Wellington evening service time of 7 p.m. was fixed to enable the Mission staff teams to reach Wellington after their Sunday afternoon's work.

- - - - - - - - - - - - - -

In 1905, the Year Book records that the Missionary Committee and the Women's Home Mission Committee were responsible for activities which included:–

At Piccadilly:

A Young Men's Society Class on Sabbath afternoons, with a Mutual Improvement Society, Swimming Club, Rambling Club, Male Voice Choir, and Recreation Class. They had a summer camp on a farm at Strachur. Sabbath Evening Services. Prayer Meetings, Gospel Temperance Meetings. A Library and Reading Room. A Mothers' Evening and Sewing Class. A Band of Hope Branch. A Penny Savings Bank. A Cripple Children's Parlour. The 32nd Glasgow Company, the Boys' Brigade.

453 children were attending the Sabbath School and 166 young people the Sabbath Forenoon Meeting. A Bible Woman was supported.

At Cranstonhill (where at that time there was less work among adults; there was no Mission congregation and there was an endeavour to reach people not attending church elsewhere):

Sunday afternoon meetings. Total Abstinence Society. "Kitchen Meetings" (with special reference to "the problem of Sharp's Lane", one of the poorest parts of the district, and being a way of reaching people who would not come to a public service). Reading and recreation rooms. Mothers' Meetings (Clothing Society and Rent Fund). Penny Savings Bank. Sewing Class. 9th Glasgow Company, the Boys' Brigade. Young Men's Bible Class. Young Women's Bible Class. Industrial Class. British Women's Temperance Association-Y Branch.

532 children attended the Sabbath School and 261 the Sabbath afternoon "Home House", a Sunday School for children up to 9 years of age.

The Women's Home Mission Committee did extensive work in the Missions with particular reference to the relief of poverty and the provision of clothing.

There was a tea party in the winter and a summer sail by steamer to Blairmore.

A typical week's programme was:–

	Piccadilly	*Cranstonhill*
Sabbath	Boys' Brigade Bible Class	Boys' Brigade Bible Class
	Children's Forenoon meeting	Children's Forenoon meeting
	Young Men's Society	Sabbath afternoon meeting
	Sabbath School (5 p.m.)	Afternoon meeting for
	Open-air meeting	working men and wives
	Evening Service	Sabbath School (5 p.m.)
		Young Men's Bible Class
		Young Women's Bible Class

Monday	Mothers' meeting and sewing class	Children's library
	Library	Industrial Class (young women)
	Industrial Class (daughters)	Penny Savings Bank
	Penny Savings Bank	
Tuesday	Cripple Children's Parlour	Mothers' meeting
	Boys' Brigade band practice	
Wednesday	Prayer Meeting	Clothing Society
		Brass Band practice
		Temperance Meeting (monthly)
Thursday	Mission Choir practice	Boys' Brigade Drill, Gym. and Band Practice
	Boys' Brigade Gym. Class and Boys' Room	
Friday	Band of Hope	Band of Hope
	Boys' Brigade Company Drill	Young Men's Gym. Class
Saturday	Gospel Temperance Meeting	
	(The Reading and Recreation Room was open nightly except Wednesdays)	(The Reading and Recreation Room was open nightly except Thursdays)

This programme of services, activities and events continued, with adaptations and changes from time to time to meet the needs of the neighbourhood.

The 19th Glasgow Company, the Girls' Guildry, started at Piccadilly in 1905/6 and the 27th followed at Cranstonhill in 1908/9.

In 1906 we read of an outing by steamer for the Cranstonhill children, accompanied by many of the Wellington Congregation, to Lochgoilhead.

In 1907 Municipal District Libraries were started, and this led to the giving up of the lending libraries at Piccadilly and Cranstonhill.

In 1920 the Sunday School figures were:

	Piccadilly	Cranstonhill
Teachers	31	49
Pupils	414	532

In 1921, the Public Health Department used the Stobcross Halls as a centre for feeding mothers and children. In the same year a Young People's Social Club was formed at Cranstonhill.

In 1926 it is recorded that a staff of 300-plus was engaged in the activities of Wellington and its two missions. The Piccadilly and Cranstonhill outings were by motor charabanc to Balfron.

In 1928 we read that the Anderston District congregation was now 378 strong. At Piccadilly the Young Men's Afternoon Class had football, swimming, rambling, and a camp in Fife; 270 mothers were attending the Monday afternoon meeting and sewing class, and 249 girls the Monday evening sewing class. The Sunday School had 475 attending, and 155 came to the Children's Church; 57 teachers were engaged. The 19th Company of the Girls' Guildry had 70, the 32nd Glasgow Company of the Boys' Brigade Bible Class had 68 and the Life Boys 50, and the B.B. had their camp at Dunure on the Ayrshire coast. The British Women's Temperance Association Y-Branch had an outing by steamer to Dunoon, while the Cripple Children's Parlour were entertained for a day at Rossdhu House on Loch Lomond.

1928 at Cranstonhill, 400 mothers attended the Tuesday afternoon meeting. There were 533 at the Sunday School (with 41 teachers), while the children's forenoon meeting on Sunday attracted 180. The 58 members of staff were appealing for helpers. The B.B. Bible Class had 45 and the Life Boys 30, while the Girls' Guildry had 52. A joint Band of Hope branch with Piccadilly had 364 members. New activities included a Recreation Club with badminton on Mondays, games on Tuesdays, and lectures and debates on Saturdays. The 9th B.B. went to camp at Macharioch near Southend in Kintyre.

In 1933, we read that the Church Sister and 150 workers were providing mission services for about 1,500 people of all ages at Piccadilly; at Cranstonhill the Church Sister and 160 workers were serving about 1,400. At Cranstonhill the work was further linked with St. Mark's-Lancefield and the Trinity College Missionary Society.

There was a Fair Holiday Camp at Troon for 35 men of the Young Men's Society for ten days at an inclusive charge of £1!

After the 1937 reorganisation into "Wellington Halls" at 185 Stobcross Street, the Year Book for 1938/39, the year before the Second World War, records:

Church Sister:	Miss Joan Mair
Choirmaster:	Andrew Archibald
Hallkeeper:	James Corlett

Sunday B.B. Bible Class, 10 a.m. 82 on roll. 18 officers, warrant officers NCOs and instructors. (See also Monday, Wednesday and Friday.)

Young Men's Society, 2.30 p.m. 118 on roll. 9 staff led by Mr. Thomas Hart.

Primary Sunday School, 2.30 p.m. 146 on roll. Leader: Miss May Swanson; Beginners: Miss Janette Copeland. Staff of 32.

Sunday School, 5 p.m. 250 on roll. Staff of 34. Superintendent: John Notman; Girls' Bible Class, 5 p.m. 84 on roll. (Teacher: Miss Farmer.)

Evening Service, 7 p.m.

Monday	Primary Playgroup, 6.30 p.m.

Girls' Club – Needlework Section, 7.30 p.m.
                    Dramatic Section, 8 p.m.
                    (See also Thursday)
                    295 on roll: Miss Farmer with 44 staff.

Men's Club. 7.30 p.m.

B.B. Band Practice, 7.45 p.m.

Penny Savings Bank, 8.30 p.m.

Tuesday   Women's Meeting, 2.45 p.m. 400 on roll. Staff 48.

Cripple Parlour (alternate Tuesdays), 6 p.m. Superintendent: Miss McCallum. 5 staff.

Badminton Club, 7.30 p.m.

Wednesday   Life Boy Team Parade, 7 p.m. 66 on roll. 9 leaders.

Mid-Week Service, 7.30 p.m.

Male Voice Choir, 8 p.m.

B.B. Gym. Class, 8.15 p.m.

Choir Practice, 8.30 p.m.

Thursday   19th Glasgow Company Girls' Guildry Parade, 6 p.m. 142 members. Guardian: Flora Campbell.

Girls' Club – Domestic Science Section, 7.30 p.m.
                  Keep Fit Section, 7.30 p.m.

Friday   B.B. Parade.

During and after the war, the need and opportunity for service diminished. The 1947/48 Year Book, reporting on this time when the mission work at Anderston was moving to its inevitable close, shows these activities still continuing:–

Sunday	*Wednesday*
B.B. Bible Class	Girls' Club
Young Men's Society	B.B. Gym. Class
Primary Sunday School	Young Mothers' Club
Sunday School	Male Voice Choir
Monday	*Thursday*
Junior Boys' Club	Brownie Pack meetings (each of two
Young Men's Society Club Night	packs still at full strength)
Girls' Club	Girl Guides parade
Tuesday	*Friday*
Women's Meeting	Play Centre
Mixed Badminton Club	B.B. parade. (Music Class,
Life Boys Parade	Ambulance Class)
	Drama Group

The building was open for table tennis, reading room and canteen throughout the week.

There was a Reunion and Social Evening on 27th March 1947 to mark the jubilee of the Young Men's Society.

- - - - - - - - - - - - - - -

These other dates may revive memories or illustrate trends.

The Boys' Brigade began its remarkable work among boys in 1883. The 9th Glasgow Company was formed on 12th October 1885 and became based at Cranstonhill, while the 32nd Glasgow started on 17th May 1886 at Piccadilly. In 1905 they had a joint camp at the public halls in Strachur, sailing there "all the way" by steamer from Glasgow. In 1907 and 1908 they had their 21st anniversary parades, when the Inspecting Officer was their founder, William A. Smith, who gave the address.

In 1923/24 the 32nd B.B. formed Boy Reserves (to become Life Boys in 1926) and in 1925 the 9th B.B. followed suit.

In 1933 – B.B. Jubilee Year – they held a combined parade on 21st April, when the Inspecting Officer was Sir A. Steven Bilsland, Bt., M.C., and there was a large turn-out of old members.

In 1935, the 9th and 32nd Companies combined as the 32nd Glasgow Company and in 1948 the company was disbanded.

88

It was not until 1940 that the 239th Glasgow Company, the Girl Guides Association, was formed on 23rd March. On 24th December 1943 the 239th Glasgow Brownie Pack was started. The 239A Pack followed on 11th September 1947 – defying the run-down of the mission! – but events overtook the devoted leaders, and of those who continued in other local premises, the 239A Pack was abandoned in 1951, then the 239th Company of the Guides in 1961, and finally the 239th Pack of Brownies in 1967.

In 1968 the records report that all Wellington's mission work in Stobcross had ceased.

- - - - - - - - - - - - - -

When the work was at its height, the Reports are filled with details of the activities, and remarkable accounts were provided by Miss Joan Mair, the Church Sister at Piccadilly from June 1925 and later at Stobcross House until she retired in January 1947, and by her opposite number at Cranstonhill, Miss Edith M. Macdonald.

The end of the Home Mission work in Anderston had an extraordinary effect on Wellington. The tradition of service sustained so faithfully was arrested, and for a long time there was an unsettled period of anxious consideration as to the role of Wellington, with particular reference to the growth of the University, where the position of Wellington was inhibited by the fact that Wellington was not the University Parish Church, and the University Chapel and Chaplaincies were engaged in work and activities among the student population.

Wellington took a long time to adjust to the new situation and to recover confidence as to its future area of active service.

Foreign Missions

From the beginning Wellington has taken an active and supporting role in the overseas work of the Church, with generous contributions and the maintaining of effective contact with missionaries.

In 1905 we read of the congregation's support of the foreign mission work of the U.F. Church in 15 mission fields – 6 in India, 1 in China, 5 in Africa, 2 in the West Indies, and 1 in the New Hebrides. It is noted that there were 314 European missionaries involved and 4200 "native agents".

It would be impossible in a book of this kind to chronicle all the types of activity and contact, but it might be of interest to list those missionaries who were connected with Wellington in some way – ex members, "Partners" some under the Partner Plan Scheme of 1962-63, and associated workers in the mission fields.

The dates are those when reference was first traced in our records.

Missionaries connected with Wellington

	1881	Miss Katherine Miller, Rajputana. First woman missionary to enrol in Zenana Mission staff; retired 1914. Died 1931. (Member)
	1904	Rev. J. W. Runciman, B.D. Udaipu.
	1905	Miss M. Amess, Akpap, Calabar, Nigeria. Adopted as Wellington's own missionary 1915-1928.
	1907	Mr. W. E. Souter, Scottish National Bible Society, China.
	1907	Mrs. Herbert A. Whitlock, American Presbyterian Mission, Lahore.
Missionary Committee (Salary paid: ½ – 2 members, ½ – congregation.)	1908	Dr. Berkeley H. Robertson, M.A., B.Sc., M.B., Ch.B., medical missionary at Bandawe, Livingstonia. Retired 1910.
Women's Foreign Mission Association	1908	Miss Mary Slessor, Old Calabar, Nigeria, "up-river station". British Consul, Okoyong Province.

MARY SLESSOR

Mary Mitchell Slessor of Calabar – Pioneer Missionary, by W. P. Livingstone (1917) tells how she was born in 1868 and died in 1915. Calabar was founded in 1846 and became a United Presbyterian enterprise in 1847. She went out in 1876 to the Bight of Biafra near the Niger delta. In 1909 the chauffeur of the government car was a member of Wellington, which was now supporting her. In 1912 the ladies of Wellington sent out a "Cape Cart" – a basketchair on wheels propelled by two boys.

Missionary Committee	1910	Rev. William P. Young, M.A., Bandawe, Livingstonia. 1912. Overtoun Institution. 1914. 9th Royal Scots. 1915. Wounded. M.C. D.C.M. 1916. Chaplain 3/5th and 4th Seaforth Highlanders (till 1919). 1922. Livingstonia.
G.A. Girls' Own Missionary	1911	Miss Janie S. Hart, Livingstonia, Ekwendeni, Nyasaland, Africa, and Madras, India.

G.A. Girls' Own Missionary	1912	Dr. Mary Alexander (or Silver), M.A., M.B., Ch.B. Ekwendeni, Nyasaland, Africa and Madras, India; from 1917. Scottish Women's Hospital, Salonika Expeditionary Force, Serbian Order of St. Save (IV Cl.), French Medaille des Epidemics.
	1914	Dr. Hubert F. Wilson (Elder 1914), M.C. and bar, Livingstonia. Grandson of Dr. David Livingstone. Medical work at Chitambo.
	1916	Miss I. McLaren Young, M.A., Bombay.
	1920	Miss A. S. Runciman, Ajmer, Rajputana. (Member)
	1920	Miss A. P. Martin, M.D. Nagpur.
	1922	Miss Anne A. Smith (nurse), Moukden.
	1924	Dr. and Mrs. Adolph Geyer, Jalna, Madras.
	1924	Dr. Margaret R. Oulton, Manchuria.
	1925	Dr. Janet S. Mackay, Manchuria.
	1926	Miss Alison F. Morrison, Gold Coast, West Africa.
	1932	Miss Winifred Shaw, Blantyre.
Missionary Society	1932	Rev. George Fraser, M.A., United Copper Belt Mission, Northern Rhodesia.
	1936	Miss Mary Carrick Anderson, Kalimpong.
	1937	Miss E. M. McGregor, Rajputana.
	1938	Dr. Mollie Hardie, India.
Woman's Guild	1940	Miss E. M. Mitchell, Manchuria, and Madras, India.
	1943	Miss Dorothy Renwick, Krobo, Gold Coast, West Africa. (Member)
	1943	Dr. David Livingstone Wilson, Livingstonia, and Inbwa, Northern Rhodesia.
	1944	Miss Betty Scrimgeour, Kalimpong, West Bengal, and Sikkim, Northern India.
Woman's Guild	1946	Miss Jean Ewan, Tumutumu, Kenya. (Mrs. Wilkinson)
Woman's Guild Partner	1948	Miss A. R. B. (Nancy) Paterson, St. Columba High School for Girls, Bombay; Women's Teacher Training College, Poona.

	1950	Miss Margaret Simpson, S.R.N., Vellore College, South India. (Member)
	1955	Rev. Kenneth MacKenzie Anderson, B.A., Wazirabad, West Pakistan. Sheikhupura, Sialkot, West Pakistan. (Member)
Partner Nov. 1962	1957	Rev. David L. Rae, B.D., Poona (Pune), Western India. (Assistant Minister)
	1957	Rev. J. (Hamish) N. Walker, B.D., Calcutta, Bengal. (Member)
	1957	Rev. Ewen G.S. Traill, M.C., Dr. Graham's Homes, Kalimpong, West Bengal.
Partner	1961	Rev. Gordon C. Morris, B.D., Kitwe, Copper Belt, Northern Rhodesia.
Partner	1964	Sister Ann W. McGoff, Wadia Hospital, Shukrawar Peth, Poona, West India.
	1965	Rev. John G. Webster, B.Sc., Kalimpong, West Bengal. (Assistant Minister)
Partners	1968	Ian and Mrs. Margaret (Hart) Coltart, Poona (Pune). (daughter of Thomas Hart)
Partner	1968	Rev. William M. Aitken, B.D., Abakalikei, Nigeria (Biafra).
	1969	J. Douglas and Grace Rogerson, Blantyre, Malawi. (Members)

Partner in Woodlands	1981	Miss Elizabeth Alexander, Kenya.

Since 1964 we have had an active Missionary Contacts Group, sending out regular letters and papers about Wellington, training material and other items. The first convener was Miss Jean L. R. Syme and the work was carried on by Dr. Malcolm Shaw and Miss Elizabeth Scrimgeour.

WOODLANDS CHURCH

94

The Woodlands Story

The union of the Congregations of Wellington and Woodlands in 1974 was a remarkable event in that both these Congregations, brought up in the United Presbyterian tradition, had their roots in the Anti-Burgher section of the Secession Church. It withdrew from the Shuttle Street congregation to a room in the Cow Loan in 1747, and then moved in 1754 to the Havannah Street–Duke Street corner, where it thrived as the only congregation in the Glasgow neighbourhood of the Anti-Burgher section of the Secession Church. As we have seen, what became the Wellington Congregation began as the separate Associate Congregation of Anderston in 1792.

The portion of the Congregation which continued experienced in 1840 certain misunderstandings. There were two collegiate ministers, the Rev. Dr. Robert Muter and the Rev. Hamish M. MacGill, and one of them, Mr. MacGill, tendered his resignation to the Presbytery, but before the resignation could be disposed of, he received a call to Airdrie. This induced some of the congregation, who were very attached to him, to promote a petition to the Presbytery on 10th November 1840 that, along with their junior minister, they might be disjoined and formed into a separate congregation. Mr. MacGill signified his concurrence with the petition, the call to Airdrie was set aside, and the new Congregation, subsequently known as Montrose Street, forthwith organised.

The original members numbered 186 including six Elders. They met in the Hall of the Mechanics' Institution in North Hanover Street for a year, but immediately obtained a suitable site for a new church in Montrose Street near the corner with George Street. A neat Gothic structure was erected from plans of Messrs. Brown & Carrick, Architects, and on their first anniversary the Congregation took occupation. The building cost about £3000 and had nearly 1000 sittings. The opening day was 10th November 1841.

The Congregation soon began to prosper and quickly cleared the debt representing the cost of their building. They took an active interest in missionary work at home and overseas.

Mr. MacGill was called away to a Home Mission appointment in 1858 and the Rev. David Young from Milnathort was inducted on 22nd March 1859. He led a significant expansion in the activities of the Congregation. A Home Missionary and a Day School – opened in 1847 and continued till the passing of the Education Act in 1872 – in the Rottenrow district were for long maintained, together with "a female missionary or Biblewoman, and a prosperous Savings Bank". There were three Sunday Schools, and Foundry Boys' meetings, "kitchen meetings", and an active band of district visitors. There was a large Missionary Committee and a Juvenile Missionary Society managed by young people, a Dorcas Society, and a special fund for the congregational poor. Strong support was given to foreign missions.

Music was led by a precentor, and the congregation remained seated during the singing.

In May 1872 the changing city led to the congregation's finding the situation of Montrose Street in many respects inconvenient. They discovered a new site in Woodlands Road at the gates leading to the former Woodlands House (hence the name Woodlands Gate), and built a handsome new church there at a cost of upwards of £15,000. It was designed in the French Gothic style by John Burnet (Senior) (1814-1901), father of Sir John James Burnet (1857-1938) and contained church hall, vestry, session and managers' rooms, waiting rooms and beadle's house. The memorial stone was laid on 21st March 1874 and it was opened on 12th November 1875. John Burnet also designed Elgin Place Congregational Church in 1856, the head office of the Savings Bank of Glasgow, the Clydesdale Bank premises in St. Vincent Street, the Stock Exchange, and Cleveden Crescent.

The church in Montrose Street was sold for £5,160.

On the occasion of the Golden Jubilee in 1890, the Rev. Robert Young, D.D., hoped the anniversary "would stimulate a general desire to make our congregational future not only worthy of its not inglorious past, but a distinct advance upon it in holy consecration, liberality and service".

As soon as the congregation was established, missionary work began in the Maryhill district in the neighbourhood of Garscube Road, and in 1898 excellent buildings were opened in Kew Street (later Ancroft Street) at a cost of £2,700. By 1903 there were 650 children and 40 to 50 teachers in the Sunday School alone, in addition to Band of Hope, Boys Brigade, Christian Endeavour, Musical Association, Mothers' Meeting, Men's Club, Penny Bank, and services on both Saturdays and Sundays.

The work in Ancroft Street continued until the early 1970's, and the Boys' Brigade company there continued under the wing of Queen's Cross Church while the 6th Girls' Brigade under Miss Winifred Hose continued in Oakbank School.

As at Wellington, Woodlands supported for several of the 1914-1919 war years two families of Belgian refugees.

The Roll of Honour contains the names of 32 men who lost their lives,

WOODLANDS CHURCH INTERIOR

including three sons of the Rev. David Woodside, who was minister of Woodlands until his death in 1924. The 1939-45 war was to add another six.

The congregation had hoped to celebrate its own centenary in November 1975, but it was not to be.

In the early part of 1973 the Kirk Session of Woodlands initiated discussions with the Presbytery's Maintenance of the Ministry Committee and with the Presbytery Clerk concerning the numerical and financial state of the congregation and the Presbytery's plans for the Church in the fast-changing Woodside area, but nothing significant emerged. A Gift Day Appeal was generously supported but it highlighted the precarious state of the congregation's finances.

Meantime Woodlands embarked on a "Woodside for God" campaign over twelve days along with members from the neighbouring congregations of St. Mary's Episcopal Cathedral, St. Silas English Episcopal Church, Park Pentecostal Church and Wellington. A course of training for visitors was conducted by Captain Stephen Anderson. Every house in the Parish and adjacent areas was visited and over 1,000 copies of the Gospel of St. John (some in Asian languages) were distributed.

In December the sad news was received that the old Woodlands Institute building in Ancroft Street, Maryhill, had been almost totally destroyed by fire.

These strands became woven into a thread of connection with Wellington's Objectives Committee, it being Woodlands' particular concern that there should be on-going missionary work in the Woodlands Parish.

On 28th February 1974, a meeting of representatives of the two churches took place at Wellington. Woodlands had 307 members left, yet was sustaining remarkable work among young people – Girls' Brigade (22), Girl Guides (27), Brownies (14), Scouts (17), Cubs (14), and the "Lotus Club" (15) for teenage immigrant girls.

It was decided that one Church, Wellington, would be used for worship, and that the Woodlands site would be continued so long as practical as a base for work in the Woodside area. The minister of Woodlands would come as Associate Minister to Wellington.

These talks gradually superseded the conversations which had been going on between the churches in the Hillhead area.

The office-bearers prepared a Draft Basis for Union, whereby the united charge would be known as Wellington Parish Church, with Wellington as the place of worship. The Church and Halls of Woodlands would be used or let or sold for the benefit of the united Congregation as they might determine in fulfilment of their role and according to their resources, to the intent that so far as possible in the light of existing needs, work in the Woodlands part of the parish would continue. The Kirk Sessions would merge, and the management of the secular affairs of the united Congregation would be under the Wellington constitution, with the neat and effective provision that at the first Annual Meeting of the united Congregation the vacancies occurring through retiral of Managers by rotation would all be filled by the election of members from Woodlands.

After approval by the two Kirk Sessions, the Basis of Union went before Special Meetings of both Congregations on Sunday 5th May 1974, where the proposals were approved, and then went to the Presbytery who received and approved of them on 14th May. On Thursday 30th May there was a Service of Union at Wellington conducted by the Presbytery and on 2nd and 9th June Communion Services were held first in Woodlands and then in Wellington.

Mr. T. B. Honeyman became joint Session Clerk at Wellington.

This happy merger, achieved with remarkable facility, increased the membership from 939 to 1,159 as at 30th September 1974, while of course the united Congregation benefited enormously from the acquisition of the Woodlands buildings and site, and the manse at 1 Manor Road in Jordanhill.

In September, a Special Meeting of the Congregation resolved to sell the Woodlands site and buildings, but not the vacant ground behind at Woodlands Gate, to the Congregation of St. Jude's Free Presbyterian Church, of 278 West George Street, for £35,000. This posed two problems in that the purchasers did not wish either the fine organ or the excellent stained glass windows.

After anxious discussion of possibilities, the organ was dismantled (much of this work being done by volunteers) and the materials sold. Thanks to the organisation of Mrs. Ella Wylie in particular, a full set of coloured and black and white photographs of the windows was taken by Doctor Robert C. Cumming. Extensive enquiries were made to ascertain the artistic and commercial value of the windows. The local planning authority was consulted about objections under the rules governing churches in conservation areas, and the families of donors were approached.

It emerged that the stained glass was of high artistic quality – particularly the five Sir Edward Burne-Jones windows in which the firm of William Morris & Co. was also involved, and forming a memorial to Mr. Peter Hamilton, a much respected member of Woodlands. It was indicated that the windows might fetch anything between £2,000 and £10,000 but the cost of removing and storage would be substantial. The Trustees therefore decided reluctantly not to exercise their reserved right to remove the windows.

(The windows were eventually removed to the District Council's historic buildings materials store, and some have been on display to the public. In October 1976 it was learned that a new church in the Gorbals was to have one of the windows showing our Lord as the Good Shepherd).

Thanks to the photographer, a fine black and white and coloured record was made for display on the Wellington Church premises and illustrations were published in the Church Notes.

The hall at Wellington was named the Woodlands Hall and a large blow-up photograph of Woodlands Church was erected there.

In 1975, the war memorial tablets from Woodlands were erected in the passage opposite the entrance to the Woodlands Hall, and the Garden of Remembrance, established in 1969 and dedicated in memory of a Woodlands member, was re-dedicated at Wellington at the north end of the garden ground.

In 1981 an opportunity came to sell the Woodlands Gate ground for £20,000 to a developer who has built 16 flats in 2 blocks of 4 storeys each on the site.

The old Woodlands Church was extensively overhauled and the stonework cleaned, revealing unexpectedly three bands of colour round the spire.

Woodlands Ministers

Rev. Hamish M. MacGill, D.D.	1840-1858
Rev. David Young, D.D.	1859-1890
Rev. David Woodside, M.A., B.D.	1885-1924
Rev. John Oswald Westwater, M.A.,	1926-1947
Rev. Alestair Bennett, T.D., M.A.	1948-1958
Rev. Ian M. Forbes, M.A.	1959-1966
Rev. John A. Grimson, M.A.	1966-1974

The Centenary Celebrations, 1984

A Centenary Celebrations Committee was appointed in January 1981 by the Kirk Session to consider suitable ways and means of recognising the centenary of the present church building in 1984. The Convener was Mr. James Michael.

Having reviewed the events of previous anniversaries and the approach of the bicentenary of the Congregation in 1992, and having regard to the present size and resources of Wellington, they decided that it would be unacceptable to be extravagant in marking the centenary, and that any cost incurred should not divert the normal giving of the Congregation from their support of Wellington itself or of the wider work of the Church. The celebrations would consist of a series of events for the Congregation and a modest enhancement of the Church buildings, to be self-supporting if possible in finance, coupled with a significant fund-raising effort to make donations to suitable projects at home and abroad.

CENTENARY GARDEN FETE STALLS

CENTENARY GARDEN FETE – HOT DOGS!

A centenary logo (shown on the frontispiece of this book) was approved and through four special bulletins under the title *Wellington One Hundred*, issued in April 1982, October 1983, and March and June 1984, the Congregation was kept advised of plans and events.

Promotions included the sale of commemorative items including a new line-drawing of the Church by Miss Sarah Swain, a large number of pottery mugs bearing the centenary logo, and attractive greetings cards with a drawing of Wellington by Walter Towers (1926).

A jumble sale on Saturday 1st October 1983 produced the satisfactory sum of £653 which was used to provide for the organisation of a Centenary Garden Fête, held in the Church and Church grounds on Saturday 2nd June 1984. The Fête was successful beyond expectations and we were blessed with a fine day. The contributions of materials for sale and the attractive setting for the event revealed the Congregation working together at its best, and from the opening at 10 a.m. by Mr. Howard Lockhart, a member of the Congregation and BBC personality, until the fête closed around 4 p.m., visitors kept coming and the supplies kept up. Stalls included books and magazines, bric-a-brac, cake and candy, arts and crafts, fruit and plants, groceries, handkerchiefs, nearly new clothing, soft goods, and a bottle stall. The "silent auction" was a notable success, and the catering a delight. The Rev. John A. Grimson and his Fête Committee had done a splendid job. The proceeds of the Lenten lunches, the jumble sale, and the Fête made possible substantial donations of £2,500 each to be made to two projects, one at home and one overseas:

1. The Lodging House Mission in East Campbell Street, Glasgow, which provides warmth, food and Christian witness for the many hundreds of folk from the East End of the city who are in need. Wellington and Woodlands over the years had assisted the Mission in many ways. The building was in a serious state of disrepair and the Mission faced heavy repair bills.

2. Pachod Village, Pune, India.

This is a comprehensive health and development project near Arwangabad in Maharashtra State in India. The first part of the project is a primary health care system to tackle the very high rates of infant and child mortality in the surrounding villages. A new 100-bed unit was opened in 1983 as the base for community health care programmes. Recognising that health is much dependent on the economic well-being of the area, the second part of the project comprises a dairy programme, an afforestation programme, and a bio-gas development, producing gas for lighting and cooking. This represents real aid, aid that actually combats poverty and is channelled towards the poorest of the poor.

The balance of the funds from these sources, together with a collection of copper coins from members, and particularly the ½p coins in course of withdrawal from circulation, and the special collection from the Centenary Communion Service (£709), and the proceeds of the Grand Centenary Concert made possible a significant donation for famine relief in Ethiopia, a cause which touched the conscience of the country after television revelations of appalling conditions in Africa.

On Sunday 8th January 1984 a new Pulpit Fall was dedicated, together with a pulpit Bible – in the New English Bible translation – which was presented by our two ministers, Mr. Craig and Mr. Grimson.

The fall was commissioned by the Committee from Mrs. Hannah Frew Paterson, a member who is an expert on fabric design and ecclesiastical embroidery. It has three main features: its background of richly varied colours: its set of twenty pillars in different shades of gold; and its dominant features of a golden half-circle embracing a smaller gold circle.

The background is made up of one hundred strips representing the hundred years of worship in the building. Fifty multi-coloured strips of silk and fifty strips of gold leather gradually merge into a single blue, the colour which stands for truth and echoes the many blue furnishings elsewhere in the Church. This multi-coloured background speaks of the great mixture of people in God's world and their presence in our parish; it declares the multi-coloured make-up of our part of the city and our opportunity to stand for the truth of the Gospel in our cosmopolitan parish.

The gold pillars represent the twenty pillars of Wellington, perhaps its most distinctive feature. They are in gold leather, but shaded in such a way that the six centre pillars stand out as the front pillars facing University Avenue stand out – the Church in the midst of its parish, proclaiming God's covenant with His people.

Lastly, the half-circle of gold leather, covering an aluminium base, reflects the many half-circles in the building – particularly those above each of the twelve windows – while the circle within it reflects the circle containing the cross on the Communion Table and that, with the dove of the Holy Spirit, behind the pulpit. The half-circle, superimposed on its stem, portrays the cup of which Jesus said, "This cup is the new testament in my blood which is shed for you". The cup embraces the circle–symbol of eternity and representing the world and all its people, and suggesting the never ending quality of eternal life which is promised to us through God's covenant, His new testament in Christ.

The cost of the new pulpit fall was met by the Woman's Guild.

The organ pipes were repainted in gold, and these features greatly enhanced the pulpit area.

A personal donation was used to purchase an upright piano to be kept in the church adjacent to the pulpit.

Meantime, the entrance from Southpark Avenue to the side door (the busier door) and the pathway between the side door and the front steps were treated with slabs and surrounded by new coloured chips, greatly improving the appearance and use of these paths.

Two special services were conducted on Sunday 4th March and Sunday 13th May 1984.

The first was a Centenary Baptismal Service to which were invited people who or whose children had been baptised in Wellington. This attracted many old friends, and after the service there was a remarkable display in the library of twenty-five christening robes provided by Wellington families and set out most attractively by Mrs. Lizanne McKerrell.

The second was a Centenary Marriages Service for people whose marriage had been celebrated in Wellington. Again there was a large attendance and the service took the form of a re-dedication. The display

INTERIOR, WELLINGTON CHURCH 1984

in the library this time was of wedding photographs of which there was a large collection.

The Recreation and Parks Department of the Glasgow District Council kindly laid out a flower bedding display in Victoria Park in June to mark our centenary.

There were three Centenary Organ Recitals on Wednesday 23rd May by John R. Turner, organist of Glasgow Cathedral, on Wednesday 19th September by Joseph G. Cullen, Master of Music at St. Andrew's Cathedral, Glasgow, and on Wednesday 17th October by George McPhee, organist of Paisley Abbey. A combined donation programme for the three recitals was produced, and these events of very high quality revealed the organ as a fine concert instrument.

The climax of all the preparations was of course the Centenary Service on Sunday 7th October 1984. The Church was well filled and many old members joined the congregation. St. Andrew's saltire flag flew on the front steps on a bright early autumn day. Guests included the Right Hon. The Lord Provost, Mr. Robert Gray and his lady; the Rev. Alexander Cunningham, the Presbytery Clerk, and Mrs. Cunningham; Mr. Alex. R. Craig, Headmaster of Hillhead High School, and Mrs. Craig; Mrs. Jane Melvin, Head Teacher of Hillhead Primary School; Miss Jean Rutherford, Headmistress of Park School; Mr. and Mrs. Geoffrey Jarvis; and the Rev. and Mrs. Stuart W. McWilliam. The Rev. and Mrs. John A. MacNaughton joined the lunch later, Mr. MacNaughton representing the Moderator of the Presbytery of Glasgow.

The preacher was the Right Rev. John M. K. Paterson, M.A., A.C.I.I., B.D., Moderator of the General Assembly of the Church of Scotland, whose wife was among the guests. He gave a delightful address to the children about his moderatorial robes and preached a powerful sermon.

The Service, for which a special Order of Service leaflet was supplied, contained a Prayer of Rededication in which the whole Congregation participated.

The Special Offering for the Fabric Fund raised £1,792.

After the service a Centenary Lunch was held in the University Refectory across the road from the Church. There, after a delightful meal, the Rev. Stuart W. McWilliam entertained the company with a humorous and pointed speech about Wellington as he saw it.

On Wednesday of that week, 10th October, a very large company of members attended a Civic Reception in the City Chambers on the invitation of the Lord Provost. After an address of welcome from the Council, the cheques for the Centenary Projects were handed over by our Ministers to representatives of the Lodging House Mission and Christian Aid. The Glasgow Phoenix Choir entertained us with a concert of choral works and solos, and a delightful supper ended this splendid evening out.

On Sunday 14th October, the Centenary Communion Service had a special note of thanksgiving for the past hundred years and rededication at the entry upon a second hundred years in the building. A special collection was taken for Famine Relief in Ethiopia (£708).

Special mention must be made of the beautiful and appropriate flower displays and arrangements at all the centenary services, for which the Flower Committee under the convenership of Mrs. Rona Thomson were responsible.

The Glasgow Tree Lovers Society kindly offered to plant a tree in the Church garden to mark the centenary and this was carried out in the Spring of 1985. A plaque commemorates the fact.

The congregation was in happy mood when a large audience packed the Woodlands Hall for a Grand Centenary Concert produced by Howard Lockhart on Saturday 27th October. This revealed an astonishing variety of talent and humour from within the congregation and formed a fitting conclusion to the events of this centenary year.

The Organ

The organ was built by Messrs. Forster and Andrews of Hull in 1884 at a cost of £1,126. The original specification provided 3 manuals and 34 speaking stops with tubular pneumatic action to the great and swell organs and mechanical action to the choir and pedal organs. The organ and its case weighed about eight tons.

Minor improvements were made in the first year and further modifications were made in 1906. In 1911/12 the blower and engine were overhauled and "noisy mechanism" repaired. Further modifications were made in 1913, and there were repairs in 1925/26.

There was a major change in 1950/51 when Rushworth and Dreaper of Liverpool carried out a raising of the central pipe feature with the tuba at the top of the apse and an increase in the number of speaking stops to 48. Pipework and tone were altered, and reeds revoiced. New keyboards were fitted, new drawstop action and new swell pedals. The pedalboard was altered to a more radial layout. The tracker action was replaced by pneumatic. Grills were inserted in the case to allow a better distribution of sound.

In 1962 the organ was dismantled and cleaned, the pedal organ was extended and tonal improvements were made.

In 1974 a report on the condition of the organ was sought from Mr. George Wilson, our organist, and the salient features of his report were published in the Church Notes in October. The organ was well provided with wind with the exception of the swell organ which often showed signs of "sagging", possibly because this department had grown out of proportion to the original 1884 specification in subsequent rebuilding.

Much of the pipework was of good quality and had remained in good condition for 90 years; the zinc pipes however did not produce a good sound and it was sometimes difficult to relate their sound to the rest of the organ. The windchests were sound and of good quality. The console was not comfortable to sit at and somewhat cramped. The keys were worn and uneven and the stop-jambs illogically placed in relation to each other. The action, by then pneumatic throughout, was deteriorating, the most off-putting feature of the instrument since the swell spoke well behind the other departments, and the pedals spoke unevenly. Mr. Wilson favoured mechanical action over pneumatic and electric action because of its reliability and durability and because it allows the player to play more expressively.

The siting of the various departments did not allow the organ to speak as a whole; the choir was directly behind the great and the pedal pipes crammed in on either side.

Dr. Peter Williams of the University of Edinburgh confirmed Mr. Wilson's views, and warned that while the organ had been built to high standards, its age was beginning to tell.

This led to anxious consideration of the possibility of building a new and smaller classical organ, but the cost was prohibitive.

A representative Organ Committee was appointed, with our organist Miss Sarah Dawe and Mr. George McPhee, organist and choirmaster of Paisley Abbey, as advisers. They reported in May 1976, suggesting four courses of action:–

1. Purchase a new pipe organ. Estimates of £35,000/£40,000 had been received for a 2-manual 25-stop classical organ, but the cost was prohibitive and the organ too small.
2. Purchase an electronic or digital organ. This proposal was not recommended.
3. Rebuild the existing organ. Tenders had been sought and Messrs. Nicholson and Company (Worcester) Ltd. of Malvern had offered £23,000 to include electrification of the whole action and the provision of a new console which could therefore be relocated.
4. Take no action, with the danger of impending collapse.

The committee recommended Course No. 3, and as reported elsewhere this was considered along with the need for fabric repairs against the background of the available financial resources. The decision was to proceed with the rebuilding in 1976/77, and there followed the interesting decision to place the console in the centre of the east gallery and not in the centre area or east transept.

The rebuilt organ has three manuals, CC to A, 58 notes and pedals CCC to G, 32 notes. There are now 44 speaking stops and 12 couplers, etc., making a total of 56 drawstops. The pitch was lowered.

Swell Organ (enclosed)

1. Tremulant
2. Swell Octave
3. Swell Unison Off
4. Swell Suboctave
5. Clarion   4
6. Trumpet   8
7. Double Trumpet   16
8. Oboe   8
9. Plein Jeu   V   rks
10. Gemshorn   2
11. Nazard   2   2/3
12. Flute   4
13. Principal   4
14. Celeste T.C.   8
15. Salicional   8
16. Rohr Flute   8
17. Principal   8

Pedal Organ

18. Schalmei   4
19. Trumpet (from 7)   8
20. Double Trumpet (from 7)   16
21. Trombone   16
22. Mixture   III   rks
23. Flute Octave   2
24. Choral Bass (from 26)   4
25. Bass Flute   8
26. Principal   8
27. Lieblich Bourdon   16
28. Bourdon   16
29. Open Metal   16
30. Acoustic Bass (from 27 & 28)   32
31. Great to Pedal
32. Swell to Pedal
33. Choir to Pedal

Choir Organ

34. Tuba   8
35. Tremulant
36. Dulzian   8
37. Cymbel   III   rks
38. Larigot   1   1/3
39. Tierce   1   3/5
40. Principal   2
41. Spitz Flute   4
42. Stopped Flute   8
43. Swell to Choir

Great Organ

44. Trumpet   8
45. Fourniture   IV   rks
46. Fifteenth   2
47. Twelfth   2   2/3
48. Flute   4
49. Octave   4
50. Stopped Diapason   8
51. Viola   8
52. Open Diapason   8
53. Bourdon (from 27)   16
54. Choir to Great
55. Swell to Great

Great – Pedal Combs. Coupled

Accessories

Six adjustable thumb pistons to Swell
Six adjustable thumb pistons to Great
Five adjustable thumb pistons to Choir
Six adjustable toe levers to Pedal
Six toe levers to Swell (duplicating)
Four general thumb pistons
General cancel piston
Reversible thumb piston for Swell to Pedal
Reversible thumb piston for Swell to Great
Reversible thumb piston for Great to Pedal
Reversible thumb piston for Swell to Choir

(*Accessories, contd.*)   Reversible toe lever for Great to Pedal
Balance Swell pedal
2 warning lights
Electropneumatic action

The organ has proved to be a successful concert instrument over the years and there have been many distinguished visiting organists.

Organ Recitals

1954	May 7, 8	Dr. Francis Jackson, Organist, York Minster.
1955	May 17	Dr. Melville Cook, Leeds Parish Church, Hereford Cathedral.
1956	May 10	Arnold Richardson, Wolverhampton Civic Hall.
1957	May 3	Catherine Crozier, U.S.A. concert organist.
1958	May 13	Noel Rawsthorne, Liverpool Cathedral.
1959	May 28	Eric Chadwick, Manchester.
1960		Margaret Cobb, London.
1963	September	Simon Preston, Sub-organist, Westminster Abbey.
1977	September 28	George McPhee, Organist, Paisley Abbey.
	October 12	George Wilson, Organist, Dunblane Cathedral.
	October 26	Simon Wright, Organist, Ampleforth Abbey.
	November 9	Dr. Francis Jackson, Organist, York Minster.
	November 23	Sarah Dawe, Organist, Wellington Church.
1978	February and March	Four promenade recitals (the Glasgow Society of Organists).
1984	May 23	John R. Turner, Organist, Glasgow Cathedral.
	September 19	Joseph G. Cullen, Master of Music, St. Andrew's Cathedral, Glasgow.
	October 17	George McPhee, Organist, Paisley Abbey.

Epilogue

It has been said that tradition depends less on what those who went before have done than on what those who follow build on that heritage. Tradition can be inspiring, but it can also be intimidating.

The congregation can be proud and grateful for the life and work of those who went before; it is for us to seek, each according to his talents, to carry on the tradition in the light of the times in which we live.

Mr. McWilliam told us at the Centenary Lunch that there is a tendency to think that in the past things were easier, but there is no evidence of this. As our Minister has said in his Foreword, "Our time is now".

It is on record that the role of a missionary congregation comprises eight key areas of action:–

1. Maintenance of services of worship;
2. Pastoral concern for the Parish;
3. Theological and related studies;
4. Teaching of the faith;
5. Development of the faithful;
6. Maintenance and development of buildings and equipment;
7. Ministry to the city as a whole;
8. Engagement in the wider work of the Church – at home and overseas.

This brief history will show how our congregation has tried to achieve these objectives. The task is ongoing.

Someone said that a congregation was simply a gathering of ordinary people inspired by the Holy Spirit to do something a little extraordinary.

Prayer does not remove our problems; it gives us strength and will to do our best to solve these problems.

Let our thoughts at this time of celebration be those which Dr. Black expressed at the Centenary of the congregation in 1892, that we should look upon this milestone "to deepen our feelings of thankfulness and of attachment to the congregation, and intensify our resolution to perpetuate and increase whatever has been good in our congregational life", and pray for the strength and will to do that together.

THE MINISTERS

Rev. John Mitchell, D.D., S.T.P., Princeton and Glasgow.   1793-1844
> Born 15th October 1768.   Inducted 1st August 1793.
> Died 25th January 1844.
> Started the Missionary Society.
> Moderator of the United Associate Synod 1825.

Rev. John Robson, M.A., D.D., Lasswade.   1844-1872
> Born 18th June 1804.   Inducted 2nd June 1840.
> Died 21st January 1872.
> Moderator of United Presbyterian Synod 1861.

(Both Dr. Mitchell and Dr. Robson died four years after
the appointment of their colleagues and successors.)

Rev. James Black, D.D., St. Andrews.   1872-1894
> Born (Duns) 1826.   Died 6th October 1913.   and
> Inducted as colleague and successor 6th February 1868.   1899-1902
> In sole charge 1872.
> Moderator United Presbyterian Church 1892.
>
> "As a preacher he was eminently scriptural and
> satisfying . . . As a pastor he excelled."

Rev. David W. Forrest, D.D.   1894-1899
> Inducted as colleague 15th March 1894.
> Translated to Wemyss Bay 1899.

Rev. George Henry Morrison, M.A., D.D., Dundee.   1902-1928
> Ordained 1894.   Inducted 13th May 1902.
> Died 14th October 1928.
> Moderator of the General Assembly of United Free
> Church 1926.
>
> "A beloved pastor and great preacher of the Word."
>
> "He was quiet in his manner, he was clear in his
> meaning, he loved his fellow men."
>
> "Our children will never forget him. He preached
> to them in sermons of flowers".

Rev. Ernest David Jarvis, M.A., D.D., London.   **1929-1958**

> Ordained 4th May 1920.   Inducted 5th June 1929.
> Retired 4th May 1958.   Died 21st January 1964.
> Moderater of the General Assembly of the Church of
> Scotland 1954.
>
> "A warm-hearted, devoted and generous man – brave
> in misfortune, humble in success, staunch in friendship
> faithful in his pastorate, forceful in his pulpit."
>
> "The streak of impishness which would invade the
> merely formal occasion only added to the superb dignity
> of manner and speech when the occasion demanded."
>
> "How beautifully he read the Bible."
>
> (Both Dr. Morrison and Dr. Jarvis were Moderators
> in their semi-jubilee years in Wellington.)

Rev. Stuart Wilson McWilliam, M.A., S.T.M., Aberdeen.   **1959-1972**

> Born December 1915. Ordained 1941. Inducted 9th
> March 1959. Called to Killearn: left 16th January 1972.
>
> "His preaching is a blend of profound spiritual
> insight and tough minded social realism that is truly
> arresting and inspiring."
>
> "His Christianity is at once robust and relevant."

Rev. Maxwell Davidson Craig, M.A.(Oxon.), B.D., Th.M.   **1973-**

> Ordained 1966.   Inducted 17th January 1973.

and since the union with Woodlands Church in 1974,
Associate Minister:–
Rev. John Alexander Grimson, M.A.   **1974-**

> Ordained 1950.   Inducted to Woodlands Church 1966.

The Ministers act as Chaplains,
Mr. Craig in Hillhead Primary and High Schools;
and Mr. Grimson at Gartnavel General Hospital,
The Queen's College, The Park School and Willowbank School.

THE ASSISTANT MINISTERS

(Note: The first mention of "official" Assistants – as distinct from students – is in 1932/33.)

Rev. H. C. Donaldson, M.A.	April 1933 – 1935
Rev. Duncan Darroch, M.A., B.D.	1935 – October 1937
Rev. Donald G. Mackintosh Mackay, B.D., S.T.M.	October 1937 – 1939
Rev. W. D. Laird, M.A.	1939 – 1941
Rev. John G. Thornton, B.A. (Oxon.).	1941 – 1943
Rev. Roderick MacIver.	1944 – 1947
Rev. J. Christian Brown, M.A.	1947 – 1955
Rev. David L. Rae, B.D.	Nov. 1955 – Sept. 1956
Rev. Charles H. H. Scobie, B.D., S.T.M.	Sept. 1956 – Dec. 1958
Rev. John Gordon Webster, B.Sc.	May 1959 – 1960
Rev. Alastair F. McCormick.	1961 – February 1962
Rev. John M. Black, M.A., B.D. (Minister Assisting).	1962 – Sept. 1963
Rev. Iain G. Nicol, B.D.	1963 – 1965
Rev. T. Q. Johnston, B.D., B.Sc. (U.S.A.)	1965 – June 1966
Rev. Sam McNaught, B.D.	1966
Rev. Saindi Chiphangwi.	Sept. 1966 – June 1967
Rev. Gordon F. C. Jenkins, B.D.	1967 – June 1968
Rev. James A. Leishman, L.Th.	1968 – May 1971
Rev. Elizabeth Newlands, B.D.	1971
Rev. Alastair Symington, M.A., B.D.	June 1971 – May 1972
Rev. W. Crawford Anderson, L.Th.	1972
Rev. Mrs. Jean (Sheena) B. Montgomerie, M.A., B.D.	Sept. – Dec. 1972
Rev. John U. Cameron, B.Sc., Ph.D., B.D.	22nd June 1973 – Sept. 1974

THE ORGANISTS

Frederick Turner (who was blind).   1884 – 1936
   Appointed 14th July 1884. Retired 31st March 1936.
   Died 12th December 1936.
   His memorial chair stands on the west side of the choir stalls.

John B. Rankin, B.Mus., L.R.A.M., L.T.C.L.   1936 – 1951
   (The organist of the University of Glasgow, A. M.
   Henderson, A.R.C.M., deputised during the war years.)

William M. Coulthard, F.R.C.O., L.R.A.M., A.R.C.M. 1951 – 1973

George Wilson, Dip.Mus.Ed. R.S.A.M.   1973 – 1975

Sarah Dawe, B.A.   1975 –

THE CHURCH OFFICERS

Mr. MacKay	1886 – 1889
James Jardine	1889 – 1900
John Herd	1900 – 1925
Alexander N. Ewing	1925 – 1955
Robert McAdam	1955 – 1963
Robert A. Wilson	1963 – 1977
Mrs. Jean Chambers	1978 –

CHURCH SISTER

Miss Agnes C. Patterson   1912 – 1946
Helped in early days of Woodlands Mission.
Started as a Bible Woman at Cranstonhill in 1912.
Appointed Church Sister 1917, and did out-
standing work in the Congregation.

CHURCH SECRETARIES

Miss J. Freda S. Anderson		1946 – 1954
	and	1955 – 1966
Miss Mary S. Waugh, M.B.E.		1966 – 1968
Miss Muriel L. Reid, D.C.S.		1969 – 1971
Mrs. Margaret Hamilton		1971 –

THE KIRK SESSION

The Session Clerks

Andrew Allison	1792 – 1826
Robert Kirkwood, Junior	1826 – 1846
George Robson	1846 – 1881
M. P. McKerrow (assistant 1876)	1881 – 1894
Alexander Fleming	1894 – 1902
Thomas Stark Brown, D.L., LL.D. (Elder 1891; Superintendent of Sunday School until 1908; Continued as Senior Session Clerk until 1938.)	1902 – 1931
Sheriff John S. Mercer (as Junior Session Clerk) (Elder 1929)	1931 – 1937
Norman Carrick Anderson (Elder 1918) } Joint {	1937 – 1958
John Strang (Elder 1941)	1952 – 1958
Professor James W. Howie } Joint {	1958 – 1961
Alfred F. Rogerson (Elder 1937) Rollkeeper 1945 – 1975	1958 – 1964
Kenneth K. Weatherhead (Elder 1949)	1964 – 1975
Tom B. Honeyman (from Woodlands Church) (Elder 1954)	1974 (joint) – 1975 and 1975 –

117

THE BOARD OF TRUSTEES AND MANAGERS

The Preses

(Mr. David Rowan was Preses at the time of the move
until after the opening services.)

J. B. Kidston	1884	Alan D. Cuthbert (Elder 1947)	1948 – 1951
M. P. McKerrow	1885	Robert Kemp	1951 – 1956
Richard Mitchell	1886	Ernest D. Webster	1956 – 1958
Albert Harvey (Elder 1902)	1889	Ian B. Rodger (Elder 1965)	1958 – 1962
Dr. Robert S. Allan (Elder 1902)	1900 – 1905	Major J. Walter M. Richmond (Elder 1960)	1962 – 1967
John Baxter (Elder 1891)	1905 – 1912	Ralph A. Hillis	1967 – 1969
William Cuthbert (Elder 1906)	1912 – 1921	William J. Renfrew (Elder 1961)	1969 – 1973
Arthur Whitson	1921 – 1924	Ronald G. Graham (Elder 1975)	1973 – 1975
Andrew Houston	1924 – 1931	James Michael (Elder 1975)	1975 – 1978
Andrew B. Fairlie (Elder 1906)	1931 – 1933	Alan N. Conner	1978 – 1981
Thomas Stark Brown (Elder 1891)	1933 – 1935	Ronald M. Kelman (Elder 1980)	1981 – 1984
William Clark Reid (Elder 1910)	1935 – 1945	Robert M. Rogerson (Elder 1965)	1984 –
Dr. James M. McNeill	1945 – 1948		

The Clerks

William Kidston	1884 – 1886
Thomas Stark Brown (Elder 1891)	1887 – 1894
Alexander Fleming	1894 – 1902
William James Mitchell (Elder 1912)	1902 – 1933
William Patrick Mitchell	1933 – 1934
Ralph Stark Brown	1934 – 1935
John McKay (Elder 1941)	1935 – 1936

Clerks (*contd.*)

Norman Carrick Anderson (Elder 1918)	1936 – 1938
George Robertson (Robin) Roxburgh	1938 – 1939
James B. Robertson (Elder 1941)	1939 – 1949
A. M. Ogilvie Robertson	1949 – 1951
Ian B. Rodger (Elder 1965)	1951 – 1956
Andrew C. Syme (Elder 1947)	1956 – 1959
Douglas L. Reid (Elder 1960)	1959 – 1963
Hugh D. B. Morton	1963 – 1964
Colin Brown (Elder 1960)	1964 – 1968
Bayne A. P. Shaw	1968 – 1972
Douglas W. F. Ferguson	1972 – 1976
Spencer F. R. Patrick	1976 – 1979
Douglas G. McKerrell (Elder 1982)	1980 –

The Treasurers

Alexander Fleming	1884 – 1905
David W. Kidston	1905 – 1909
Patrick H. Aikman (Elder 1902)	1909 – 1921
Robert G. Millar	1921 – 1924
Arthur Whitson (Elder 1933)	1924 – 1935
Lindsay M. Scott (Elder 1937)	1935 – 1944
W. Maxwell Simmers (Elder 1937)	1944 – 1960
Thomas W. Donald	1960 – 1963
David D. R. White (Elder 1952)	1963 – 1967
James S. Whitelaw (Elder 1967)	1967 – 1975
William B. Duthie	1975 – 1978
Mrs. Wilma Hainsworth	1978 – 1981
Miss G. A. Rose Chillas	1981 –

THE MISSIONARY SOCIETY AND MISSIONARY COMMITTEE

Presidents
The Ministers
Vice-Presidents

Dr. Robert S. Allan (Elder 1902)	1905 – 1921
John Baxter	1921 – 1924
William Cuthbert	1924 – 1945
John P. Sutherland	1946 – 1952
Mrs. W. L. McKerrow	1950 – 1951
John Strang	1951 – 1952
Mrs. Lois C. Jarvis	1952 – 1958
Alfred F. Rogerson (Elder 1937)	1956 – 1968
Thomas Hart	1957 – 1968

Executive Committee (1962) – Chairmen

Ralph A. Hillis (Elder 1965)	1962 – 1966
A. N. R. Steel (Elder 1956)	1964 – 1968
Dr. Malcolm Shaw (Elder 1960)	1968

Treasurers
(covering home missions and foreign missions)

N. Carrick Anderson (Elder 1918)	1905 – 1906
Patrick H. Aikman (Elder 1903)	1906 – 1909
Steuart Anderson (Elder 1916)	1909 – 1933
W. L. McKerrow (Elder 1908)	1909 – 1919
J. McGregor Hart (Elder 1922)	1913 – 1917
Andrew Houston (Elder 1938)	1918 – 1939
John Walker (Elder 1938)	1929 – 1946
William J. Hill	1931 – 1932
W. Maxwell Simmers (Elder 1937)	1932 – 1937
David S. Sligh (Elder 1947)	1943 – 1956
John Blair (Elder 1947)	1946 – 1953
Miss Annie F. Silver	1951 – 1958
David Watson (Elder 1949)	1953 – 1964

James S. Whitelaw (Elder 1967)   1958 – 1967
Miss May W. Swanson (Elder 1969)   1959 – 1964
Charles Mathieson (Elder 1975)   1967 – 1968

PROJECTS COMMITTEE (after 8th April 1968)
(Formerly Executive Committee of the Missionary Committee)
Conveners

Dr. Malcolm Shaw (Elder 1960)	1968 – 1969
William C. Brown (Elder 1960)	1969 – 1974
Professor John Aitchison (Elder 1969)	1974 – 1976
J. Douglas Rogerson (Elder 1969)	1976 – 1977
Edward Harvie (Elder 1964)	1977 – 1979
Dr. Stuart G. Hoggar (Elder 1980)	1980 –

WOMEN'S HOME MISSION COMMITTEE
Presidents

1905 – 1913	Mrs. James Young
1913/14 – 1928/29	
	Mrs. Wm. Cuthbert
1929/30	Miss Farmer

WOMEN'S FOREIGN MISSION ASSOCIATION
Presidents

1905 – 10	Miss Mitchell
1910/11 – 1928/29	
	Mrs. G. H. Morrison
1929/30	Mrs. P. H. Aikman

Vice-Presidents

1910/11 – 1928/29	
	Mrs. P. H. Aikman
1911/12 – 1923/24	
	Miss Howden
1921/22 – 1928/29	
	Mrs. M. P. McKerrow
1929/30	Mrs. A. Houston

(Miss Greta S. D. Carrick Anderson was Treasurer for Foreign Missions from 1912 till 1930, and continued in the Woman's Guild until 1945/46.)

THE WOMAN'S GUILD (from Wednesday 12th March 1930)
(new constitution 1952/53)

Presidents

1930/31 – 1947/48	Mrs. Elizabeth H. McKerrow (also National Guild President 1943 – 1947)
1948/49 – 1957/58	Mrs. Lois C. Jarvis (also National Guild President 1951 – 1955)
1958/59	Mrs. Winifred Howie
1959/60 – 1962/63	Mrs. Jessie Dingwall (also National Guild President 1955 – 1959)
1963/64 – 1966/67	Mrs. Mary Walker
1967/68 – 1969/70	Mrs. Margot McWilliam
1970/71 – 1972/73	Miss Janette W. Copeland
1973/74 – 1975/76	Mrs. May Anderson
1976/77 – 1978/79	Mrs. Mary Hill
1979/80 – 1981/82	Miss May W. Swanson
1982/83 – 1984/85	Mrs. Janet Craig

Vice-Presidents
(I – Standing Committee for Home Missions;)
(II – Standing Committee for Foreign Missions)

1930/31 – 1933/34	Miss A. Farmer (Convener I)
1930/31 – 1931/32	Mrs. P. H. Aikman (Convener II)
1932/33	Mrs. Patrick (Convener II)
1932/33 – 1933/34	Mrs. A. Houston (Convener II)
1934/35 – 1941/42	Mrs. J. Syme (Convener I)
1934/35 – 1939/40	Mrs. Stella Hart (Convener II)
1940/41 – 1947/48	Mrs. May Buchanan (Convener II)
1942/43 – 1950/51	Mrs. Jean Boyle (Convener I)
1948/49 – 1950/51	Mrs. Nora Stark Brown (Convener II)
1951/52 – 1953/54	Mrs. Jean Murdoch (Convener I)
1951/52 – 1954/55	Mrs. Rita Cumming (Convener II)
1954/55 – 1955/56	Miss Kathleen Aikman (Convener I)
1955/56 – 1957/58	Mrs. Winifred Howie (Convener II)

1956/57 – 1959/60	Mrs. Jean Sligh (Convener I)
1958/59 – 1961/62	Mrs. Mary Walker (Convener II)
1960/61 – 1963/64	Miss Jean L. R. Syme (Convener I)
1962/63 – 1965/66	Miss Mina C. MacLeod
1964/65 – 1967/68	Miss J. Freda S. Anderson
1966/67 – 1968/69	Mrs. Julia Shaw
1968/69 – 1971/72	Mrs. Kathleen M. Gray
1969/70	Miss Janette W. Copeland
1970/71	Mrs. Mary Martin
1971/72 – 1973/74	Mrs. Mamie Young
1972/73 – 1974/75	Mrs. Mary Hill
1974/75 – 1976/77	Mrs. Margaret Muirhead
1975/76 – 1977/78	Mrs. Amelia Alexander
1977/78 – 1978/79	Miss May W. Swanson
1978/79 – 1980/81	Mrs. Jean Weir
1979/80 – 1981/82	Miss Jean L. R. Syme
1981/82 – 1983/84	Mrs. Nelly Galloway
1982/83 – 1984/85	Miss Elizabeth Scrimgeour
1984/85 –	Mrs. Mamie Young

THE CONGREGATIONAL SUNDAY SCHOOL

Superintendents

William McKerrow (Elder 1858)	⎫ Combined service	1856 – 1912
William L. McKerrow (Elder 1908)	⎰ over 78 years	1909 – 1933
David J. D. MacBrair (Elder 1929)		1933 – 1935
James A. Crawford (Elder 1921)		1935 – 1944

Philip A. Beattie (Elder 1967)	1976 – 1984
Stephen W. Pearson	1984 –

Primary Department

Superintendents:

Miss Milne	1912 – 1917
Miss Boyd	1917 – 1918
Miss Helen Cairns	1918 – 1923
Miss Elsie Mitchell	1923 – 1925
Miss Helen H. Simmers	1925 – 1927
Miss Agnes M. Houston	1927 – 1930
Mrs. Helen Cairns	1930 – 1931
Miss Nancy Morton	1931 – 1935

Leaders:

Miss Jean L. R. Syme	1935 – 1949
Miss Janette W. Copeland	1949 – 1950
Miss Mary M. Pryde	1950 – 1951
Miss Janette W. Copeland	1951 – 1968
Miss Elizabeth Logan (Mrs. Thomson)	1969 –

Beginners Department

Leaders:

Miss Jean L. R. Syme	1932 – 1935
Miss Dorothy J. S. Renwick	1935 – 1941
Miss J. (Peggy) McCaskie	1941 – 1944
Miss Mary B. Rodger	1946 – 1955
Miss Marjorie Bosomworth	1955 – 1960

Miss Frances C. MacCallum	1961 – 1962
Miss Margaret Arthur	1962 – 1972
Miss Christina Galloway	1972 – 1977
Miss Henrietta Wilson	1977 – 1980
Miss Jane Penrice	1980 – 1981
Mrs. Jane Grimson	1981 –

Under 4 or Pre-Beginners

Leaders:

Mrs. C. H. H. Scobie	1957 – 1958
Miss Morven Gray	1958 – 1961
Miss Helen Steven	1962 – 1963
Miss Catriona Ross } Miss Carolyn Anderson }	1963 – 1964
Miss Susan Rankin	1964 – 1965
Miss Marjory Syme	1965 – 1970
Miss Winifred Kerr	1965 – 1972
Miss Susan Bennie	1970 – 1972

Miss Henrietta Wilson	1974 – 1977

Junior Department

Superintendents:

Mrs. W. Cuthbert } Miss May S. McKerrow }	1918 – 1919
Miss Margaret E. A. Aitken	1919 – 1920
Miss Margaret L. Shields	1920 – 1922
W. L. McKerrow (interim)	1922 – 1923
Miss Jean M. Semple	1923 – 1925
Miss J. M. Macdougall Ferguson	1925 – 1927
Miss Emma G. Haggart	1927 – 1928
Miss Jean M. Humphreys	1928 – 1935

Leaders:

Ronald B. Neill	1935 – 1937
Miss Edith M. Hunter	1937 – 1944
Mrs. Isobel Gibb	*1945 – 1946
Miss Katherine E. Humphreys	1946 – 1953
Miss Margaret F. Sinclair	1953 – 1957
Miss Dorothy Thomson	1957 – 1960
Miss Marjorie D. Bosomworth	1960 – 1963
Miss Margaret Cumming	1963 – 1964
Adam Horsburgh	1964 – 1970
Philip A. Beattie	1970 – 1976
Stuart Hoggar	1976 – 1977
Ronald Slater	1977 –

*In 1941/42 until 1945/46 the Junior and Senior Departments combined.

Senior Department

Leaders: The Superintendents, and:–

Miss Edith M. Hunter }	*1941 – 1944
Brian J. F. Fiddes	*1942 – 1945
Brian J. Fiddes	1946 – 1947
W. Cecil Carrick Anderson	1947 – 1975

(He died on 11th October 1975 after a lifetime of service to Wellington. He played the organ for services on many occasions).

Philip A. Beattie	1975 – 1977
James Ritchie	1977 – 1979
Philip A. Beattie	1979 – 1984
Stephen W. Pearson	1984 –

*   In 1941/42 until 1945/46 the Junior and Senior Departments combined.

Bible Class

Leaders: The Ministers, and:–

Miss Kathleen Aikman	1933 – 1939
Rex B. Shepheard	1933 – 1935
W. Maxwell Simmers	1935 – 1939

Guy Brownlie			1952 – 1953
John Buchanan			1953 – 1954
J. R. Wallace Orr			1954 – 1957

Fred M. Walker			1960 – 1965
W. Crawford Anderson			1965 – 1967

THE YOUNG PEOPLE'S SOCIETY (Started 1937/38)
(from June 1976, THE YOUTH FELLOWSHIP)

Presidents

Rev. Donald G. M. Mackay	1937 – 1938
Miss Christina Anderson	1938 – 1939

John P. Copeland	1946–47	J. Douglas Rogerson	1966–67
Ian B. Rodger	1947–48	Tom Graham	1967–68
Hector M. McKerrow	1948–49	Suzanne Hart	1968–69
Christopher F. Strang	1949–50	Alistair Richmond	1969–70
Albert Copeland	1950–51	Neil Maxwell	1970–71
Geoffrey L. Jarvis	1951–52	Christina Galloway	1971–72
Marjorie D. Bosomworth	1952–53	Eileen Jenkins	1972–73
Robert Hill	1953–54	James Ritchie	1973–74
D. Bruce Weir	1954–55	Graeme Muir	1974–75
Michael Jarvis	1955–56	Ann Crawford	1975–76
Alexander Jarvie	1956–57	Gavin Grimson	1976–77
John Webster	1957–58	Scott Harvie	1977–78
John G. R. Howie	1958–59	Jane Penrice	1978–79
Anne Mackenzie	1959–60	Simon Aitchison	1979–80
J. Neil Barclay	1960–61	Stephen Pearson	1980–81
Peter W. Howie	1961–62	Wilma Smith	1980–81
J. Douglas Weatherhead	1962–63	Stephen Manners	1981–82
Alan S. Andrews	1963–64	Angela Cusack	1981–82
Eleanor Graham	1964–65	Andrew Pearson	1982–83
Herbert Runciman	1965–66	Andrew Peregrine	1983–84

Uniformed Organisations

6th Glasgow Group, the Scout Association

Group Scout Leader – Douglas Waddell	1974 –
Cub Scout Leader – Mrs. Gillian Dinsmore	1975 – 1983
– Mrs. Jinty Waddell	1983 –
Scout Leader – Dr. Callum Traquair	1977 – 1981

210th Glasgow Company, the Girl Guides Association

Guide Guider – Mrs. Heather McMillan	1974 – 1975
– Miss Caroline Letton	1975 – 1976
– Mrs. Catherine Beattie	1976 –
Brownie Guider – Mrs. Catherine Slater	1974 –

THE HOME MISSIONS

PICCADILLY

Sabbath School Superintendents

Thomas Stark-Brown	– 1901
Robert Millar	1901 – 1908
D. B. Murray	1908 – 1921
W. Muir Connor	1921 – 1924
Kenneth M. Sloan	1924 – 1931
John Notman (Elder 1933)	1931 – 1936

Sabbath Forenoon Meeting/Children's Church
Chairmen

John R. Fleming	1904 – 1907
John Calderwood	1907 – 1909
James Reid	1909 – 1915
Andrew J. Small	1915 – 1921
James Smith	1921 – 1936

Girls' Sewing Class/Girls' Industrial Class
Superintendent

Miss Farmer	1910 – 1936

Mothers' Meeting
Presidents

Mrs. M. P. McKerrow	1929 – 1933
Mrs. Aikman	1933 – 1936

19th Glasgow Company, The Girls' Guildry
Guardians

Mrs. A. E. Black (Acting)	1905 – 1908
Miss Jean Milligan	1908 – 1910
Miss E. M. Allan	1910 – 1918
Miss Joie Maclean	1918 – 1924
Miss Isobel G. Maclean	1924 – 1933
Miss Eileen A. Mitchell	1933 – 1936

Young Men's Afternoon Class
(Young Men's Society from 1931:–
celebrated its jubilee 27th March 1947)

Leader

Thomas Hart (Elder 1925)	1924 – 1936

32nd Glasgow Company, The Boys' Brigade
Captains

Alex. Fairlie	1886 – 1891
James F. Farmer	1891 – 1894
James P. Trotter	1894 – 1896
John B. Kidston	1896 – 1905
John R. Fleming	1905 – 1910
James Reid	1910 – 1919
George Fullarton	1919 – 1920
William Farmer MacLean	1920 – 1923
George Gareth Calvert	1923 – 1929
William Roy Farmer	1929 – 1936

CRANSTONHILL
Sabbath School Superintendents

John Baxter	1886 – 1924
Andrew B. Fairlie	1920 – 1932
Joseph Taylor	1925 – 1928
James Brown Mowat	1932 – 1933
Lindsay M. Scott	1933 – 1936

Sabbath Forenoon Meeting
Chairmen

Andrew P. Davidson	1904 – 1913
William Davidson	1913 – 1915
John R. Haddy	1917 – 1936

Industrial Class/Girls' Sewing Class
Superintendents

Mrs. Mylne	1904 – 1907
Miss McEwan	1907 – 1915
Mrs. Joseph Taylor	1915 – 1922
Miss Taylor	1922 – 1927

Mothers' Meeting

Mrs. Wm. L. McKerrow	1929 – 1936

27th Glasgow Company, The Girls' Guildry
Guardians

Miss E. M. Allan	1908 – 1918
Miss Jean C. Allan	1918 – 1919
Miss H. Constance Campbell	1919 – 1925
Miss Neta C. Christie	1925 – 1931
Miss Mary Cunningham	1931 – 1932
Miss Margaret A. G. Richardson	1932 – 1936

(continued as 19th Glasgow)

9th Glasgow Company, The Boys' Brigade
Captains

William Kidston	1885 – 1894
Andrew B. Fairlie	1894 – 1900
William L. McKerrow	1900 – 1904
W. Neislon Martin	1905 – 1906
John E. Lyle	1906 – 1919
Ian M. Grant	1919 – 1920
John B. Morrison	1920 – 1922
James K. Cuthbert	1922 – 1923
Malcolm A. Allan	1923 – 1931
Alan D. Cuthbert	1931 – 1934
J. G. W. Lee	1930 – 1936

COMBINED MISSION IN STOBCROSS HOUSE
("WELLINGTON HALLS")

Sunday School
Superintendent

John Notman	1936 – 1948

Primary Sunday School
Leaders

Miss May W. Swanson	*1936 – 1945
Miss Janette W. Copeland	*1945 – 1949
*(after service at Cranstonhill since 1928)	

Girls' Sewing Class/Girls' Club (1937)
Superintendents/Presidents

Miss Farmer	1936 – 1943
Mrs. Boyle	1943 – 1948

Children's Church
Chairman

Dr. Charles H. Moir	1936 – 1937

Women's Meeting
Presidents

Mrs. Wm. L. McKerrow	1936 – 1943
Mrs. J. Syme	1943 – 1949

19th Glasgow Company, The Girls' Guildry
Guardians

Miss Margaret A. G. Richardson	1936 – 1937
Miss Flora Campbell	1937 – 1939

Young Men's Society
Leader

Thomas Hart	1936 – 1948

32nd/9th Glasgow Company, The Boys' Brigade
Captains

J. G. Watson Lee	1936 – 1938
W. Roy Farmer	1938 – 1940
David Watson	1940 – 1948

239th Glasgow Company, The Girl Guides Association
Captains

Miss P. Goldie	1940 – 1941
Miss C. S. Clark	1941 – 1945
Miss Jean K. Stark Brown	1945 – 1949

239th Glasgow Brownie Pack (and 'A' Pack)
Brown Owls

Miss Jean L. R. Syme	1943 – 1967
Miss R. Monaghan	1946 – 1949

"They shall grow not old as we that are left grow old; age shall not weary them nor the years condemn; at the going down of the sun and in the morning, we will remember them."

"Their name liveth for evermore"

WELLINGTON CHURCH WAR MEMORIALS
1914 – 1918

Harry T. Andrew	2nd-Lieutenant	H.L.I.
J. Elliot Black, M.C.	Lieutenant	R.A.M.C.
R. M. Stewart Boyd	Lieutenant	H.L.I.
R. R. Boyd	2nd-Lieutenant	Scottish Rifles
James Brock		Cameronians
R. Stanley Stark Brown	2nd-Lieutenant	H.L.I.
Waldo Hastie Cameron	2nd-Lieutenant	Cameron Highl'rs
William Campbell Clark	2nd-Lieutenant	A. & S.H.
Robert Craig		Cameron Highl'rs
Robert Davidson		K.O.S.B.
William McKenzie Davie		Black Watch
John K. Dron	2nd-Lieutenant	H.L.I.
R. G. C. Duncan	2nd-Lieutenant	A. & S.H.
Robert Hunter Dunn	Lance/Corporal	R.Sc. Fusiliers
Ernest Blair Dymock	Sergeant Major	Canadians
Herbert Meikle Dymock	Staff/Sergeant	75 Bde. R.F.A.
Andrew Struthers Foster		Gordon Highl'rs
Alistair I. S. Fraser		Cameron Highl'rs
John McIntosh Graham	Engineer	H.M.A.T. A.37
Robert A. Gunn		Can. Exp. Force
Thomas Harvey	2nd-Lieutenant	The King's Own
Gordon R. Hay		H.L.I.
William Hayman, D.S.O.	Major	R.E.
William R. Hutchison	Captain	R.S.F.
Donald Fisher Jackson	Lieutenant	Hussars
James P. Logie	2nd-Lieutenant	Gordon Highl'rs
W. J. Lowe	Gunner	M.M.G.
Norman G. Lowson, M.C.	Captain	R.E.
George C. McEwan	Lieutenant	R.A.F.
George Lammie McEwan	Captain	H.L.I.
James Macfarlane	Gunner	R.G.A.
Donald Mackintosh, V.C.	2nd-Lieutenant	Seaforth Highl'rs
Malcolm M. Macleod	Captain	R.A.F.
John Mann, jnr.		Can. Highl'rs

John D. Milne	Corporal	Scottish Rifles
Alexander W. Morrison	Lance/Corporal	Gordon Highl'rs
Roderick E. Morrison		Aus. Imp. Forces
Graham Nelson	2nd-Lieutenant	R.A.F.
James Morris Poe	Pilot	R.A.F.
Gordon Reid	2nd-Lieutenant	K.O.S.B.
T. B. Seath McGregor-Robertson	Lieutenant	R.N.
Henry I. Runciman	Sergt./Ins.	M.G.C.
William Watson Runciman	Corporal	R.A.F.
Charles M. Sclanders	Lieutenant	O.W. Rifles
Robert Sclanders		P.P.C.L.I.
David Steel		R.A.M.C.
Andrew Sturrock	2nd-Lieutenant	R.S.F.
Archibald C. Taylor	2nd-Lieutenant	N.Fus.
Fred Taylor	Sergeant	85/Canadians
Fred W. Turner	2nd-Lieutenant	Scottish Rifles
A. R. Walls		Royal Scots
William C. Watson	Lance/Corporal	H.L.I.
R. W. Gordon Webster		Gordon Highl'rs
John Selkrig Whitson		Black Watch

1939 – 1945

William M. Aikman	Flight Sergeant	R.A.F.V.R.
Ian M. Anderson	Lieutenant	R.N.
George E. Bailey, D.S.O.	Lieut.-Comndr.	R.N.V.R.
William C. Borris	Gunner	R.A.
Richard Wallace Brown	Sergeant	Royal Signals
Alexander J. A. Buchanan	Sub-Lieut.(A)	R.N.V.R.
Neil C. Campbell	Captain	Mon. Regiment
William L. Craig	Corporal	R.A.S.C.
William A. Dickie	Surg.-Lieutenant	R.N.
Robert E. Duff	Lieutenant (E)	R.N.R.
David C. Eadie	Gunner	R.A.
Kenneth J. Ingram	Captain	H.L.I.
James Ernest Jarvis	Captain	Mahratta L.I.
George A. McCaskie	Captain	M.C.S., Att. Indian Army
John H. McCrindell	Engineer	M.N.
John Makins	Sub-Lieutenant	R.N.V.R.
Robert M. Nelson	Lieutenant	Cameronians Att. Para. Regt.
John Neville	Private	A. & S.H.
William A. Ross	Sgt.-Pilot	R.A.F.
James M. Talman, D.F.C.	Flight-Lieut.	R.A.F.V.R.
Jack M. Young	Lieutenant	A. & S.H.

1914 – 1918

Peter Crerar	5th Cameronians
D. McK. Davie	5th Cameronians
John Dick	R.C.A.
James D. Herbertson	R.N.V.R.
John T. Holland	9th H.L.I.
Richard Lauder	1st R.S.F.
Harold T. Leask	7th Royal Scots
Joseph McAdam	6th Seaforths
William McCall	9th H.L.I.
Peter W. McCarroll	R.A.S.C.
W. John McDonald	1st R.S.F.
Archibald McLachlan	5th Cameronians
Allan G. Marshall	17th H.L.I.
W. A. Mollison	6th D. of W. Reg. M.G.C.
John Mollison	R.A.F.
Alfred Motteler	6th H.L.I.
J. Noel Nelson	R.N.A.S. R.A.F.
George Porter	3rd A. & S.H.
William Robertson	M.M.G.C.
W. G. Robertson	Gordons, M.G.C.
Charles Russell, D.C.M.	46th Canadian Inf.
Gordon M. Smith	9th H.L.I.
J. Douglas Smith	7th Cameronians
Gordon Walker	R.N.V.R.
R. J. Walker	1st Gordon Highlanders
William Walker	10th Cameronians
Colin W. Walker	5th L.N. Lancs.
Frank McE. Watson	M.G.C.
David C. Woodside	4th R.S.F.
Hugh M. Woodside	9th H.L.I.
Archibald M. Woodside	9th H.L.I.
Charles S. Workman, M.C.	Cameronians, R.F.C.

1939 – 1945

Andrew Coulter Barr	R.A.F.
Arthur Beaumont Muir Crawford	Cameronians
Peter Jones	A.A.
Kenneth Martin	6th H.L.I.
Archibald Johnston Mackinnon	R.E.
William G. Reid	R.N.
John Robertson, D.F.M.	R.A.F.
David J. Woods	R.N.

Acknowledgments

Wellington Church is indebted to many people whose individual and collective contributions of information and records have made possible the compilation of this story.

Many present and past members of the congregation made available individual collections and memorabilia of all kinds and many of these kindly agreed that their items should be retained with the Church archives, which is greatly appreciated.

In addition, the following persons and institutions made significant contributions:

The Mitchell Library, Glasgow Room (City of Glasgow District Council).

The Museum of Transport, Glasgow Museums and Art Galleries.

Strathclyde Regional Council Archives, (now located in the Mitchell Library).

The Archivist of the University of Glasgow.

University of Strathclyde, Department of Architecture & Building Services.

The Church of Scotland Advisory Committee on Artistic Matters.

T. & R. Annan & Sons Limited, whose collection of Glasgow photographs is unique.

Sarah Dawe, our organist.

Geoffrey L. Jarvis.

The Rev. J. Leslie Goskirk of Lairg.

Dr. Robert C. Cumming for photographs.

Miss Mary B. Rodger who typed the entire text from the manuscript.

Mr. T. B. Honeyman who saw the book through the press.

Thanks are due for the extensive information in
A Hillhead Album: Henry Brougham Morton (Hepburn Trust)
and *Architecture of Glasgow*: Andor Gomme and David Walker
(Lund Humphries)

WELLINGTON STREET U.P. CHURCH.

PROPOSED NEW BUILDINGS HILLHEAD.

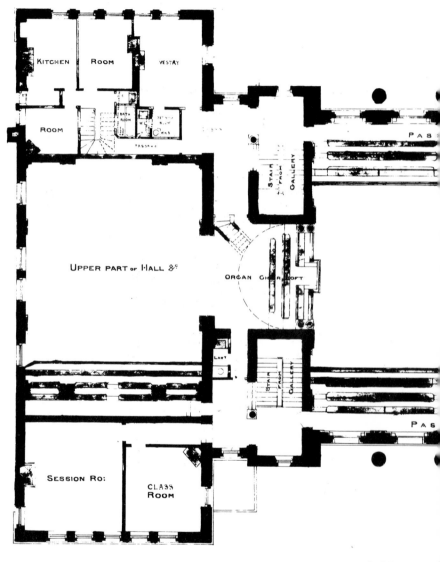

KITCHEN   ROOM   VESTRY

ROOM

BATH
ROOM

PASSAGE

UPPER PART of HALL &c

STAIR FROM GALLERY

ORGAN CHOIR LOFT

LAVY

STAIR FROM GALLERY

SESSION RO:

CLASS
ROOM

PAS

PAS

PLAN OF